CLIMBING SELF-RESCUE
Improvising Solutions for Serious Situations

If you like adventure, sooner or later you are going to help an injured partner. If you are a big-time adventurer, the injuries are going to be complicated. To help you think of solutions when in a pickle, consider reading *Climbing Self-Rescue*...Much of the book is technical, but everybody can find an idea.

—Idaho Falls Post Register

Should be on the shelves of any serious, regular climber.

—Midwest Book Review

Gem of a book...Its backpack-suitable size and laminated cover make it appropriate for field or armchair use.

—Wilderness Medicine Magazine

A must-read...The easy-to-read book illustrates step-by-step procedures for everything from passing knots through belay devices to rope-soloing safely to rescuing an injured leader. Those with a working knowledge of rope management and anchor systems can understand the techniques.

—Rock & Ice

MOUNTAINEERS
OUTDOOR EXPERT
series

CLIMBING SELF-RESCUE
Improvising Solutions for Serious Situations

Andy Tyson and Molly Loomis

THE MOUNTAINEERS BOOKS

THE MOUNTAINEERS·BOOKS
is the nonprofit publishing arm of The Mountaineers,
an organization founded in 1906 and dedicated to the exploration,
preservation, and enjoyment of outdoor and wilderness areas.

1001 SW Klickitat Way, Suite 201, Seattle, WA 98134

© 2006 by Andy Tyson and Molly Loomis

First edition: first printing 2006, second printing 2008, third printing 2009, fourth printing 2011, fifth printing 2014

Manufactured in the United States of America

Acquiring Editor: Christine Hosler
Project Editor: Mary Metz
Copy Editor: Julie Van Pelt
Cover and Book Design: The Mountaineers Books
Layout: Peggy Egerdahl
Illustrator: Mike Clelland
Photographs by Molly Loomis and Andy Tyson unless otherwise noted.

Cover photographer: Mark Fisher
Frontispiece: *The need for self-rescue skills can arise when least expected.*

Library of Congress Cataloging-in-Publication Data
Loomis, Molly, 1977-
  Climbing self-rescue : improvising solutions for serious situations / by Molly Loomis and Andy Tyson.—1st ed.
      p. cm.
  Includes index.
  ISBN 0-89886-772-X
  1. Mountaineering—Search and rescue operations. 2. Mountaineering accidents. I. Tyson, Andy, 1968- II. Title.
  GV200.183.L665 2005
  796.5'220289—dc22
                              2005035066 .
                              CIP

ISBN (paperback): 978-0-89886-772-5
ISBN (ebook): 978-1-59485-158-2

Contents

CHAPTER 7
Passing Knots

CHAPTER 8
Scenarios and Solutions

CHAPTER 9
Getting Outside Help

Acknowledgments

An enormous thank-you for the information, experiences, and time generously shared by Mike Clelland!, Kelly Cordes, Kevin Emery, Mark Fisher, Will Gadd, Ben Gilmore, Tony Jewell, A.J. Linnell, Nick Lewis, Allen O'Bannon, Jen Pine, Andy Rich, Louis Saas, Toby Schmidt, Phil Schneider, Clyde Soles, Garth Willis, and folks at the following organizations: Werner Braun (Yosemite Search and Rescue); Colby Coombs (Alaska Mountaineering School); Lisa Gnade (DMM); Mike Gibbs (Rigging For Rescue); Gordy Kito and Maureen McLaughlin (Denali National Park); Tom Moyer (Salt Lake Country Search and Rescue); Ken Phillips (Grand Canyon National Park); Kolin Powick (Black Diamond Equipment Ltd.); Paul Roderick (Talkeetna Air Taxi); Jim Ewing and Paul Niland (Sterling Rope); Jed Williamson (AAC's *Accidents in North American Mountaineering*); Julie Van Pelt (JVP Editing); Christine Hosler and Mary Metz (The Mountaineers Books). (Organizations are listed for identification only.) And our parents!

Introduction: Why Self-Rescue?

Climb long enough and at one point or another getting stuck in a jam high up off the ground is inevitable: stuck ropes, a crucial piece of gear missing in action, wandering off-route into dicey terrain, or an injury that leaves a climber in need of help. Typically, we piece or puzzle our way to a solution and move forward. Climbers are generally smart and resourceful, able to handle challenging situations, so why a whole book on self-rescue techniques?

Flip through the annual *Accidents in North American Mountaineering (ANAM)* and some obvious trends become evident. Most, if not all, climbers strive to climb in a safe, intelligent, and independent manner, but we often up the ante when we climb with less-experienced partners, fail to practice our rescue techniques (until the crucial moment), forget that we are smart and act dumb, or we end up just needing to learn the hard (sometimes very hard) way. There are plenty of accidents every year

that *ANAM* does not cover; in fact most accidents included are documented because there was outside help provided for the party. Many accidents are never reported because the climbers were able to take care of themselves, using their problem-solving, first-aid, and rescue skills to handle the situation independently.

With a little more know-how and practice, many of the reported accidents could be handled better by the party in the mountains or on the rock. The more effectively you as a climber are able to control the situation (e.g., by getting your partner safely down the route to the base of the climb rather than waiting midroute for rescue by an outside party), the less effort (and risk) is required of outside rescuers. Depending on the situation, by employing self-rescue skills you may be able to eliminate the need for outside assistance entirely, if outside assistance is even an option. Depending on weather, local resources, and your location,

Good rescue skills can minimize or eliminate the need for outside help.

it may not be. Organized rescue efforts are time-consuming, people- and gear-intensive, and are often costly, not to mention risky for rescuers (frequently volunteers). A solid grasp of self-rescue skills helps everyone in a bad situation. Remember that novice partners may find themselves needing to rescue you if things go awry. This book is not just for you; it is for your partner as well.

NUTS AND BOLTS

Climbing: Self Rescue seeks to inform readers how to confidently handle rescue scenarios ranging from simple to complex in all mediums of the vertical world—rock, snow, and ice—and also aims to serve as a resource by sharing technical tips and tricks, resources for continuing education, and data regarding both climbing-related injuries and climbing gear. It is our hope that this type of information, which helps further your skill base, can help prevent you from getting into trouble in the first place.

This is not a text on prevention of accidents; on the contrary, it assumes that you may find yourself in a situation that requires good critical thinking and creative rope work to alleviate. Prevention is, however, an overall goal, and one way to learn about prevention is to realize the penalty of failure. Understanding the reality of the real-life situations presented in this book will make any smart climber focus on prevention.

As in life, in climbing there are often multiple ways to solve a single problem.

Certainly some solutions are more efficient than others and each has benefits and downsides; but the bottom line is that the "best" solution is the one that you as a rescuer can execute successfully and safely. In writing this book we have tried to avoid a black-and-white approach to explaining rescue skills (i.e., using words like "always" and "never"). A dogmatic teaching style only hinders development of the critical thinking we believe is so important to being a competent, confident, and safe climber.

Realize that in some instances you may not agree with our approach to a certain scenario or skill; rather than discard the solution presented, take it as a learning opportunity to investigate the pros and cons of the different methods. Not every solution known to the climbing discipline is included—space, time, and sanity intervened—but we have tried to present a variety of solutions, addressing the pros and cons of each. Initially the number of options may overwhelm a climber new to self-rescue. Stick with it and all should become clear with time!

Perhaps most importantly, *Climbing: Self-Rescue* seeks to develop your critical-thinking skills as a climber. The unfortunate truth is that real-life rescues rarely unfold as in practice; the list of variables is endless. *Climbing: Self-Rescue* addresses these variables by using scenarios that call on readers' understanding of improvisational rescue. Although experience is undoubtedly one of the best teachers for developing judgment, the climbing conundrums shared in this book will help you be all the more prepared for the unexpected when it crops up.

WHAT THIS BOOK IS NOT

Climbing: Self-Rescue is not an introductory climbing manual. We assume that readers already have knowledge of and adequate practice with the following skills: belaying, rappelling, placing artificial protection, constructing multidirectional anchors, lead-climbing theory, and basic climbing knots (figure eight series and overhand series). This is also not a first-aid manual. Although some scenarios may reference specific injuries, covering the treatment, packaging, and management of such injuries is outside the scope of this book. *Medicine for Mountaineering* by James Wilkerson or the compact *Backcountry First Aid and Extended Care* by Buck Tilton are recommended as accompanying references for first-aid skills.

HOW TO EFFECTIVELY USE THIS BOOK

Chapters 1 through 7 are an instruction manual focusing on improvised self-rescue. Text, illustrations, and photographs explain knots and *raising systems,* descent and ascension methods and considerations, passing knots, how to safely assist and rig an injured climber, and a variety of other information. The simplest way to complete any given task is presented first, then other options follow.

Do you have to be a master climber to understand this stuff? No. The situations presented are easy to envision and the systems build on each other. We do not recommend jumping into something like *counterbalance rappelling* (chapter 4) right off the bat, though. The instructions in this book build on one another, so a start-to-finish read is recommended. If you know your knots (chapter 2), you may choose to start with escaping a belay (chapter 3) and work from there. The building blocks of self-rescue are all in escaping a belay and are used in conjunction with all other systems.

After the instruction portion of the book, we give you a chance to test your skills in chapter 8. This chapter is devoted to climbing scenarios ranging from moderate to severe. We asked friends and other experienced climbers for tales of their own mini and full-blown epics. Some scenarios have been tweaked a bit to illustrate a certain point, but all are from real situations. The simplest and most time-efficient solution is presented, with other options following. We also discuss potential pitfalls and prevention tips, as well as list what skills to review. More experienced readers may choose to begin with the scenarios, using the referenced sections as a way to brush up on their skills.

Information provided in chapter 9 and in the appendixes is an excellent way to arm yourself with even more knowledge. Reviewing the statistics of documented accidents over the past fifty-plus years (Appendix A) will tune you in to common accident factors, how to avoid them, and what sort of self-rescue techniques you could employ should you encounter them. Appendix B, Gear Specifications, looks at a wide selection of gear on the market and describes things like the strength of a piece of protection, a carabiner, or of webbing. Appendix C, Knot Efficiencies, can help you make conscious choices about the knots you use instead of relying on habit and memorization (as many of us do). The Continuing Education and Recommended Reading appendixes are a collection of organizations, publications, and courses that can help you continue developing your skills.

But most importantly, practice the rescue systems we describe! The only way to learn them is by practicing. Learn to use friction hitches, releasable hitches, and backups. Learn the ins and outs of raising systems. Remember: If you are in a rescue situation, things have already gone wrong. There is no good reason to shortcut safety during a rescue; you will only endanger your own life as well as your partner's. This book's goal is to help prepare you for the unexpected and practice is essential for doing just that. Just as backcountry skiers practice transceiver searches and whitewater kayakers work on rolls, climbers should practice vertical rescue skills.

Rescue is as much an art as it is a science and it is constantly evolving. We have done our best to provide accurate facts, figures and techniques but changes are inevitable. Please send your comments to us, care of the publisher, so we can keep the information current. Thanks!

A NOTE ABOUT SAFETY

Safety is an important concern in all outdoor activities. No book can alert you to every hazard or anticipate the limitations of every reader. The descriptions of techniques and procedures in this book are intended to provide general information. This is not a complete text on self-rescue technique. Nothing substitutes for formal instruction, routine practice, and plenty of experience. When you follow any of the procedures described here, you assume responsibility for your own safety. Use this book as a general guide to further information.

—*The Mountaineers Books*

CHAPTER 1

Knowledge of self-rescue techniques can help you move beyond the basics and travel with increased confidence in the high mountains.

The Basics

Bitterroot Range, Montana

John put his light gloves down on the small ledge and they promptly blew away—just another glitch in the day's long chain of events. He and his partner, Glen, had started climbing the Perfect Buttress route in Blodgett Canyon at 9:45 AM that late-September morning. The pair took their time climbing; it was a beautiful day and they were enjoying the adventurous, high quality, and seemingly remote route. They swung leads; Glen started, so he would lead the last, ninth pitch, rated 5.11. The beginning pitches had some 5.9 and 5.10 moves, so both climbers were working hard throughout the day. They arrived at the last pitch around 5:00 PM. It would not get dark until after 7:00 PM, so they did not even discuss the time. Glen was excited for the challenge; he had wanted to climb this route all season. He racked and started up.

The pitch was steep and beautiful—a combination of face and crack climbing, the high crux a thin finger crack. Glen placed some small stoppers at the beginning of the pitch, saving his cams for the crux. The lead took awhile. He rested whenever he could, trying to maintain his strength for the challenge above. John was belaying Glen with an ATC off his harness while watching some evening clouds roll in.

Glen reached the crux at about 110 feet above John. About 10 feet below the crux Glen had placed a poor nut (expecting to put a lot of good protection above). About 8 feet below that was a large cam behind a block, and 5 feet below that was a quality large nut. Glen was disappointed with the protection possibilities when he arrived at the thin crack. It was steep and the crack was narrow and bottoming. He wished he had his small stoppers! Instead he placed a small rigid-stem Friend. Since the crack was so shallow, the head of the cam was against the back of the crack and the stem pointed straight out of the rock. It did not look like there would be much more protection for another 10 feet above the piece, but the climbing did not look as hard as he had anticipated. Glen continued up. With his feet just above his last piece, he tried to find a stance for his next placement. This is where he popped off the route.

The fall was clean at first, but the rigid stem on the Friend snapped so fast that he did not even slow down. The stopper launched and then the cam disintegrated the block. Glen ended up hanging from the quality nut. He hit his head and broke his ankle and upper arm in the 65-foot fall. John launched up off the ledge and came tight to the anchor. John was now in charge of a rescue. He looked at his watch: 6:00 PM.

The steep walk-off at the top of the climb did not seem a likely option. On the route there were fixed rappel anchors at the belays since many climbers rappelled before the last crux pitch. John lowered Glen as far as he could. Because of the protection failures Glen almost reached the belay ledge. John tied Glen off to his belay device and tossed him their second rope, with a figure eight on a bight tied on the end with a locking carabiner clipped to it. Glen clipped this to his harness belay loop and then clipped the rope into the nearest piece of lead protection he could reach. Glen was able to one-handedly wiggle in a second piece for backup. John put the second rope on a Munter hitch belay and slowly released the lead belay line, making sure as Glen came tight on the second rope that the pieces held. John released the lead rope, and continued to lower Glen to the belay ledge. On the ledge he tied Glen in and started treating his injuries.

Glen was dazed but helpful. After a slow tandem rappel John decided to lower Glen to the next anchor and have him clip in while John set up a rappel for himself. The process was efficient but still somewhat slow and it was getting dark. They had to switch back to tandem rappels for the bottom pitches since they were lower angle and John needed to support Glen and his injuries. At the last rappel station John set his gloves down in haste and they blew away. The clouds he had noticed earlier were turning into a storm. He was glad they were almost back to their packs where they had some extra supplies.

At the bottom of the route John bundled up Glen in all the extra clothes and rain gear they had and helped him to a sheltered spot. John left him with water and food before turning on his headlamp and hiking the 2 miles to the road to call for help. Local search and rescue was mobilized and they used a wheel litter to transport Glen to the ambulance at the road head late that night.

ANALYSIS

Glen chose to lead a hard pitch late in the afternoon after a long day in a remote setting. Perhaps he could have worked to get better gear placements and certainly should not have trusted his highest placement. After the accident John handled the situation very competently. He improvised a system (that was creative and backed up) to get Glen back to the belay ledge. He modified his descent systems to balance speed and comfort. John organized the rescue to minimize external involvement, getting to the bottom of the cliff and making sure Glen was comfortable and stable before heading for help.

Luckily, more often than not as climbers, we deal with snafus and not incidents as serious as the one described above—like realizing midrappel that the rope ends are hopelessly uneven or needing to assist a partner through a challenging section because that person lacks experience or has a minor injury. These situations can be solved with ease and efficiency by employing a variety of simple techniques and tricks of the trade. Thankfully the "femur fracture, concussion, broken ribs, hanging from a wall 2,000 feet up, dark with a lightning storm approaching" rescue experience is not the norm for the majority of us. That said, a simple snafu can quickly turn into a full-blown emergency if it is not handled quickly and correctly. Cold, wind, weather, impending dark, altitude, and human error, compounded by a simple glitch (or a serious accident) can quickly result in a downward spiral of hypothermia, frostbite, dehydration, or mistakes made out of exhaustion.

Run back through the incident described above and imagine how the evening might have unfolded differently if John or Glen had at any point panicked, thereby losing the ability to effectively problem-solve on the spot; or if they forgot any of the basic rescue skills they successfully used to safely extract themselves from the situation. This well-managed accident could have quickly turned into a cascade of follies with perhaps a grimmer outcome.

EMERGENCY PROCEDURES

"Emergency procedures" form the organizational framework we use to deal with any critical situation. Climbing: Self-Rescue focuses on the technical skills and improvised thinking needed to effect a rescue with an emphasis on backcountry settings, but it is certainly worth taking a look at the larger foundation underlying technical rescue. You may know every rope trick in the book, but unless you can incorporate your technical skills into the bigger picture, your tricks will not do much good (and may run the risk of making the situation even worse). The following steps will help you organize the rescue, thereby helping to produce a calm and efficient operation. Not all these steps are pertinent to every situation, though they are all worth considering.

- Plan ahead and prepare (the "Five Ps": prior planning prevents poor performance)
- Assess the scene (safety for you, other rescuers, and the patient)
- Initiate first aid if necessary
- Make a plan
- Rescue
- Follow through

PLAN AHEAD AND PREPARE

Self-rescue is much easier (both logistically and mentally) if you are prepared for it. Planning ahead and preparing (also one of the seven Leave No Trace principles) are of utmost importance.

Whether a one-day outing or a month-long expedition, some initial research and basic knowledge will pay off if things go awry. Who should you call if you have a medical emergency at a trailhead? Who should you call if you need technical rescue assistance?

- Know the location of nearby public phones.
- If carrying a cell phone, know whether and where it will get coverage.
- Know the location of nearby medical facilities.
- Find and carry with you important local numbers (emergency services [911], police, local search and rescue (SAR) group, medical facilities, friends who could lend a hand).
- Leave a copy of your itinerary (route description and estimated return information) with family or friends; consider whether your route description references geographical features that will be recognized and understood by non-climbers.

Also under "plan ahead and prepare" is packing any needed supplies in the event of an emergency. A first-aid kit should be carried, even if it is just a roll of tape and some gauze pads. Hopefully you have a more comprehensive one in your pack at the base of the climb or in your car not too far away. Rescue gear is important as well (though in this book we try to demonstrate how to effect a rescue with little extra gear); it is certainly nice to have at least the basics presented in the "Equipment" section later in this chapter.

ASSESS THE SCENE (SAFETY)

Before you dive into any rescue, make sure the scene is safe for you and the patient. If there are threats to your life (e.g., loose rock, lightning, avalanche), you should make a decision that does not create more patients. This may mean waiting for the situation to change and not helping your partner immediately, a difficult yet important choice. If the scene is unstable (e.g., there may be a second round of rockfall ready to dispatch), perhaps you can quickly move the patient to another area for treatment. This move may not be the best for the patient, but it will allow you to provide care instead of you both being seriously threatened had you not made a quick move.

INITIATE FIRST AID

Not all rescues require first aid. If this one does, take it on or, if available, enlist the help of someone else. Consider whether monitoring vital signs is necessary; if so, start recording. We recommend that all backcountry travelers have a basic understanding of wilderness first aid. There are several good training institutions listed in appendix D, Continuing Education.

You do not necessarily need to be with the patient to initiate first aid. If he is conscious you can call to him to obtain information about his condition and suggest things he can do while you make a plan. However, if your partner's condition is unstable, or he is unconscious, you will need to provide hands-on care.

MAKE A PLAN

During a rescue it is tempting to just move forward with the next step without stopping the action to create a plan. This constant motion can be effective, though it can also quickly go bad. When faced with a rescue situation, stop and make a plan. The "stop" does not have to be long, but the plan should be thorough, otherwise you run the risk of wasting time and energy with unnecessary additional steps.

Once you formulate a plan, it helps to make it verbally clear. That is, you would be able to tell someone else what you have done, what you are doing, and what you will do after that, followed by why it is a good plan over other possibilities. We recommend talking the plan out even if there is no one there to hear it. This should not make you feel like you are adding sudden insanity to the list of things that are going wrong; by verbalizing your plan you are clarifying what is rapidly speeding through your head. Taking the time to justify it over other options also helps you explore other possibilities. If you realize another good option while talking it through, don't be afraid to flex your plan, though make sure it all fits together before executing it. Talking out the plan can be done with the patient as well.

RESCUE

Hopefully your rescue is simply hauling your friend up a few feet through a difficult *crux* or exiting down a route to escape an impending thunderstorm. The simple and straightforward solutions are what we are striving to help with in this book. Though we spend time in this "Emergency Procedures" section talking about the big-picture framework, this same framework can and should be pared down and applied to specific components of any situation you find yourself in. For example, say while climbing a multipitch route your partner has taken a bad lead fall and is knocked unconscious. The emergency procedures process can be implemented for each stage of the overall rescue: reaching your partner, safely descending the route, evacuating yourselves to further care from the cliff base. Each stage will have its own microplan with unique and specific details.

Outside help. In making your plan, first assess whether you can handle the situation on your own or if you should consider asking for outside help from a rescue team or from others in the immediate vicinity. If you are able to execute the rescue on your own, formulate a plan and get cracking!

If you need outside help, decide on the most effective means of contact: Using a cell phone? Sending a messenger? Leaving your patient and heading out on your own? Before involving others you should assess the situation, evaluating what is wrong and what you think should be done, and then you should make a careful decision about who you think can help. Chapter 9 goes into detail about getting outside help.

Hopefully you will be able to take care of things on your own, but know where and who to turn to in case you do need help. There are some excellent resources for rescue out there, and knowing how to access the one you need will help complete this step of enlisting outside help quickly.

In the United States, calling 911 will connect you to a local dispatcher. The dispatcher will take information from you and contact the appropriate public assistance (e.g., ambulance, sheriff, fire department, SAR, backcountry rangers).

With this call you are requesting help and when the dispatched unit arrives they will take charge of the situation. This assistance is generally welcome and helpful, though depending on your situation and the local assistance available, you may realize you could have completed the rescue a different way. For example: You are a beginner climber and your partner accidentally drops the rope while threading the rope for rappel at the anchors atop a very hard sport climb. He ends up stuck, hanging from an anchor 75 feet up a 300-foot cliff. You know your expert climbing buddy is supposed to show up in an hour and he could help you out, but you call 911 instead. The local SAR crew shows up with ten people and more on the way. They place five bolts at the top of the cliff to rap down and pick your friend off the anchor. The newspaper writes another article about crazy climbers and interviews the local landowner who again questions whether he should allow climbing on his property.

Certainly this is an overdramatization, but this book is about personal resourcefulness. We are not advocating that you take matters into your own hands if you can't handle a situation, but we are saying you should take matters into your own hands that you *can* handle.

It is worth mentioning that with *definite exception*, many SAR teams are not comprised of technical climbers. Ideally they may have a few specialized high-angle rescue technicians, but this is not always the case. Realize too that safety systems built by organized rescue teams are a bit different than the improvised rescue systems acceptable for you and your buddies; SAR teams typically work with a higher margin of safety, which can mean more gear and additional lines. This does not mean one form of rescue is better or worse than another, rather that it is important as a climber relying on outside services to be aware of what that realistically may entail. With very rare exception is a rescue just like in the movies; do not expect helicopters diving in and whisking the injured party off a cliff face.

An important resource not to overlook (particularly in the example earlier of the dropped rope at a sport crag) might be other climbers at the cliff. There are plenty of documented cases of overzealous "experts" making the situation worse, but there are plenty more cases of Good Samaritans helping others out of a bind. This is a judgment call. Maybe that day at the cliff you see some people that you know are experienced big-wall climbers, able to handle this situation. Some random folks that you have seen in the local climbing gym a few times may not be the place to turn.

FOLLOW THROUGH

The rescue is not over until you clean it up and talk about it, no matter how simple or serious the situation. This is important.

Relax and regroup before continuing. You created a little system to pull your partner up through a crux section of the climb. Although certainly not a "serious rescue," don't just launch up the next pitch; there is still valuable information to be gained that will make your climbing more efficient. Check in and make sure he wants to continue (or understands why you both need to continue) and discuss how you might make the system better if you need it two pitches up on the hardest part of the route. Another example: You just spent the last fifteen minutes yelling and doing rope tugs to let your partner know he was on belay and could start climbing. Talk about the communication gap when you get back together (even if you are at the top of the climb). It will help greatly the next time the situation arises.

Transfer the patient to someone with higher medical training. Maintain the patient as best you can while you are in charge of him. Keep track (write down if you can) how you found him, how his vitals have changed over time, and all pertinent information you can gather. This information will be invaluable for the next caregiver. Consciously transfer the patient to someone with higher medical training when that person arrives, and provide the information you gathered.

Remove rescue equipment and clean the area. Say you request a helicopter rescue for some severely injured climbers. Twenty SAR team members respond and execute the rescue. Ask them to help you clean up the area when done (if they have not already) or organize a local climber cleanup.

Evaluate. Find out what caused the accident and let your climbing friends know so they do not make the same mistake. If you have been part of a more serious incident, posttraumatic stress syndrome can be a very real, legitimate aftereffect. See the Continuing Education and Recommended Reading appendixes for references on this topic. If an organized SAR team or ambulance service is involved, they typically will have their own "critical incident stress debrief." Ask them for ideas of local resources.

WHAT ABOUT THE TEN ESSENTIALS?

If you have spent time outside you have probably heard of the Ten Essentials: ten items you should not head off into the wilds without. These include map and compass, sunglasses and sunscreen, extra clothing, headlamp or flashlight, first-aid supplies, fire starter and matches, repair kit and tools, extra food, extra water, and emergency shelter. However, considering the necessity of traveling light and fast on a route, emergency supplies realistically will vary greatly depending on the distance from car to route and from car to medical facilities, the type of route you are climbing (single pitch, long multipitch, or remote alpine route), and the type of environment you are climbing in (desert, isolated waterfall ice) and your familiarity with the area. Here are some lightweight emergency items worth considering depending upon your objective:

- **First-aid kit.** A half roll of tape in your pack or a few long strips stuck on the inside of your helmet can do wonders.
- **Knife.** Useful for cutting improvised bandages out of clothing strips. Has other very important applications, like cutting cord or webbing to leave at anchors, clearing crispy old rappel webbing, or cutting stuck ropes.
- **Space blanket.** There are several lightweight versions that fold up into extremely small packages.
- **Signal mirror.** Stranded high on a cliff this may be your best bet for signaling for help.
- **Cell or satellite phone**. Although the purpose of this book is to help make you self-sufficient in the vertical world, it would be unrealistic to discard some climber's desire and some situation's need for outside help. Realize that getting help in vertical terrain is not an immediate process. It is time-consuming, resource-intensive, and may endanger the lives of others coming to your aid. That said, cell phone coverage is constantly expanding. A cell or satellite phone is a resource worth considering for adding to your toolbox as long as it is used responsibly.
- **Small stove.** Depending on the season, length of route, and your experience level, you may consider bringing a small, lightweight stove for melting water or emergency heat.

TECHNICAL RESCUE SKILLS OVERVIEW

Technical rescue skills fit into the "Make a Plan" and "Rescue" sections of the emergency procedures framework discussed above. Although in practical application, rescue skills will typically be combined, or transitioned from one into another, for simplicity's sake this book discusses one element per chapter and then looks at how they fit together in chapter 8, Scenarios and Solutions. The following skills are covered:

- Rescue knots (chapter 2)
- Escaping a belay (chapter 3)
- Descending (chapter 4)
- Ascending (chapter 5)
- Raising (chapter 6)
- Passing knots (chapter 7)

As mentioned in the Introduction, rescue, like climbing, is open to many interpretations, systems, and opinions. Though as individuals we may think our way is the best and only way, it is neither. As the saying goes, there are many ways to skin a cat. The most important thing is that you execute these skills safely and successfully without injuring you or your partner. In each chapter we describe a safe and acceptable method of applying a skill. Then we present additional options and encourage improvisation in the scenarios later in the book.

While discussing each skill we cover common terms and language used subsequently

Fig. 1-1. An example of the basic gear that can be used to carry out an improvised rescue.

in the introduction of other skills. For that reason each skills chapter should be read and learned in order, if only so you do not miss terms that may be undefined in later skill instruction. Skills are ordered in a logical progression for learning, covering the necessary and easiest options first then moving to the more complex and less desirable options. Without a common language and understanding of rescue (just like climbing), it will be more difficult for you and your partner to work together in a tough situation.

EQUIPMENT

The beauty (and danger) of improvised self-rescue is that you are relying on yourself and no one else to carry out a safe and successful rescue. The improvisational element refers to the fact that no one, especially you, expects a need for rescue in the first place. Therefore fancy (and expensive) search and rescue gear like PMPs (*Prusik-minding pulleys*), brake bars, or litter baskets are left out of the equation. All skills taught in this book use the same items typically found on a climbing rack: a rope, carabiners, slings, and cord. Sure, items like pulleys and ascenders are certainly helpful and can make a big difference; but most of us do not typically carry that equipment on a single-day free climb. We will touch on the use of some more specialized gear (like pulleys and *mechanical ascenders*), but in general, instruction will focus on simpler tools (fig. 1-1 shows basic gear).

It is important to understand the added forces introduced in rescue situations and the limitations of climbing gear. This type of information is highlighted in sidebars throughout the book and in appendix B, Gear Specifications. Don't just assume that because a piece of gear works for climbing, it will automatically be adequate for all rescue applications.

Below is a list of gear we assume each climber will have (or each climbing party if specified). This list is an ideal; the reality is that not all climbers (especially the follower) will choose to have all of these items on his or her harness at all times. The more you learn the more you will be able to improvise and make do with what you have.

- one single *dynamic rope* per party, 50–60 meters (160–200 ft)
- six nonlocking carabiners
- six locking carabiners

HALF AND TWIN ROPES

Some climbers prefer using either a half-rope or a twin-rope system for alpine and ice endeavors. These skinny two-rope systems are lighter, can reduce rope drag, and provide a great deal of versatility. Leading on twin ropes involves clipping both ropes through all pieces of placed gear. Half-rope technique involves alternating which rope is clipped through the gear. With either system, leaders are belayed on both ropes simultaneously. Per manufacturers' recommendations, half and twin ropes are meant to be used in tandem, never by themselves.

There are no cut and dried rules for incorporating half and twin ropes into improvised rescue. Although the skinnier your rope is the less ideal it is for rescue, there are plenty of other good reasons for using skinny ropes. The biggest risk is the amount of wear and tear a half or twin rope can handle compared with a single rope. If lowering, raising, or counterbalance rappelling, take particular note if your ropes are running over any sharp edges. Use your best judgment to problem-solve and play it safe.

- forty feet of 7-millimeter accessory cord cut into five lengths
- Some webbing for creating runners
- Tubular belay device (like an ATC)
- UIAA-rated harness
- UIAA-rated helmet

ONE DYNAMIC CLIMBING ROPE

Length and diameter is left to personal preference, though considering this book focuses on single-rope technique the rope chosen should be rated as a single rope. Many climbers prefer 60-meter ropes for the versatility it allows in route selection and rappelling.

We will often refer to a second rope, although it is not necessary to purchase one simply for practicing purposes. Two ropes are needed for rappelling many routes. You can save weight and money by buying a second rappelling rope that is either of smaller diameter or that is *static* instead of dynamic. (Be aware there are specific precautions that must be taken when tying two ropes of different diameters together.)

SIX NONLOCKING CARABINERS

All UIAA-approved varieties of nonlocking carabiners are acceptable. It is not necessary to always reserve six unoccupied carabiners solely for the purpose of a rescue. If in a pinch, gear can always be reracked to free up additional carabiners.

SIX LOCKING CARABINERS

Large pearabiners are ideal for rescue applications. However many climbers scoff

Fig. 1-2. Carabiner gates are opposite and opposed, minimizing the chance of the rope slipping free should one of the gates accidentally open.

(with good reason) at the idea of carrying six locking pears; although ideal for smooth rope management and belay anchor construction, they are heavy! If you want to keep it light, try a combination of lighter weight, smaller locking carabiners and pears. Opposite and opposed nonlocking carabiners can always be used if you are stuck without enough lockers (fig. 1-2).

CORD AND WEBBING

Recommended cord and webbing lengths follow. We do not recommend that you carry all of these lengths at all times. These lengths are great to practice with and, after realizing what is most essential to various situations, you can carry various combinations of them depending on your route and conditions. With a knife the longer cords can become whatever length you need in an emergency. And with practice the shorter ones will be useful for every situation.

CORD

Cordelettes are lengths of nylon accessory cord (also called Perlon) at least 6 millimeters in diameter (there are also a few specialty cord materials on the market for cordelettes). Length can vary but they are generally at least 15 feet long. If used for linking pieces in a multidirectional anchor, a cordelette is often at least 20 feet long.

What we call a *rescue loop* is a short loop of 7-millimeter cord tied with a Flemish bend or double fisherman's. A 4-foot length of 7-millimeter cord tied off with a bend will yield a 1.5 foot long loop that makes a nice length for tying most *friction hitches;* the resulting excess loop is fairly short after it is tied on the line.

See appendix B, Gear Specifications, for more information.

Cord lengths:

- Two pieces, 4 feet (122 cm) each, tied with a double overhand (aka double fisherman's) knot (we call these rescue loops (RL); usage detailed throughout the book)
- One piece of cord as long as you are tall plus 6–12 inches (for a *waist Prusik,* detailed in chapter 5, Ascending)
- One piece of cord twice your height (for a *foot Prusik,* detailed in chapter 5, Ascending; can also double as a shorter cordelette)
- One piece about 15 to 20-plus feet (460 cm) (for a cordelette)

WEBBING

Below are some common lengths for tying runners (aka slings). See appendix B, Gear Specifications, for descriptions of the different webbing materials available. Many climbers prefer lighter weight $^{11}/_{16}$-inch webbing for slings compared to 1-inch tubular webbing. The type of route you are climbing will typically dictate what assortment of slings you decide to take. Bringing a few hand-tied slings (as opposed to sewn runners) is a good idea; they are easy to adjust, easy to thread around natural features, and can be cut up and used for creating anchors at rappel stations.

Webbing Lengths (Before Knots):

- 5.5 feet (168 cm): Single sling (draped diagonally across torso)
- 9.5 feet (290 cm): Double sling (doubled and worn diagonally across torso)
- 13.5 feet (410 cm): Triple sling (tripled and worn diagonally across torso)

BELAY AND ANCHOR TERMINOLOGY

Here are some common terms and abbreviations used throughout the book specifically relating to anchors. Protection placement and anchor-building techniques are not covered. See the Recommended Reading and Continuing Education appendixes for ideas.

BELAY POSITION

Belays can be configured off of a climber's harness as well as directly off of an anchor. Both situations are covered throughout the book and we will also touch upon the specifics of belaying with a redirectional.

Generally, lead climbers belay their second off of the anchor in good-quality multipitch rock. Belaying is done off of the harness in most other climbing situations. It is almost always easier to effect a rescue if the belay is on the anchor already, but that is not justification for belaying off of a marginal or poorly positioned anchor. Cases can be made that it is safer to belay one way over another in different situations (see appendix E, Recommended Reading for more information). Generally, we assume that a Munter hitch or a *self-blocking belay device* is used to belay off of an anchor, and any preferred belay device is used off of a harness. Knowledge of how to execute rescues from all belay configurations, including belays with a redirectional, will only increase your improvisational arsenal. We do not recommend belaying off of an anchor with a traditional stitch plate or *tubular belay device* (like an ATC) because of the upward lock-off motion these belay devices require to create an effective brake.

HANDS-FREE

How to get *hands-free* is covered in the first step of escaping a belay, in chapter 3. This basically means tying off the climber so that as the belayer/rescuer you can use both hands to complete a task rather than maintaining a brake hand. There will

Fig. 1-3. When creating a shelf, make sure to clip the carabiner in a way that includes a strand from each piece of protection used in the anchor, and have a carabiner (regardless of whether it is weighted) clipped through the master point.

be times throughout the rescue scenarios where it is possible to do something without getting both hands free first. This is certainly up to rescuer judgment. We recommend the conservative (and slower) approach at first, but as you get comfortable with the systems it might be preferable to maintain your belay with one hand and complete a few steps with the other.

ANCHORS

Multidirectional anchor. At least three solid pieces of protection, with at least one piece maintaining the integrity of the whole anchor against multidirectional pulls, including upward and sideways.

Directional anchor. At least three solid pieces of protection that are joined to create a solid equalized anchor, generally resisting a downward pull, though it might be oriented to resist an upward or sideways pull in certain situations.

Master point (MP). This is the term we use for the redundant, equalized, clip-in point of any anchor. We use the abbreviation "MP" when referred to repeatedly.

Shelf. When building an anchor it is possible to consciously create a *shelf*—a separate space to clip through just above the MP that can be as redundant and effective as the MP itself. This separate clip-in can help keep things organized and also helps keep ropes from binding up while raising or lowering. If one or two ropes are weighted and moving through carabiners next to each other, they create friction against each other and it becomes harder to move them. Physically separating the carabiners on the same anchor allows the rope to move more freely, thus reducing the loads on the anchor. *Important note:* A shelf must be equalized, and redundant; take care to clip through a section of cord coming off each piece of protection (fig. 1-3). Always keep a carabiner clipped through the MP even if that carabiner is not holding any weight; this carabiner safeguards against inverting the MP knot. A shelf should also not jeopardize the anchor in any way.

RESCUE OVERVIEW

A rescue is highly situation-dependent. The following charts are not foolproof, but they will help familiarize you with the different components of self-rescue and will help you visualize the rescue process. The charts are based on a rescue situation involving two people, one being injured. Because every situation is unique, continued improvisation and thought are necessary. Use these charts as a map to clarify and provide a basis for your thought process when entering a rescue situation and as useful reminders as you work your way through the scenarios in chapter 8 of this book.

RESCUING THE FALLEN LEADER

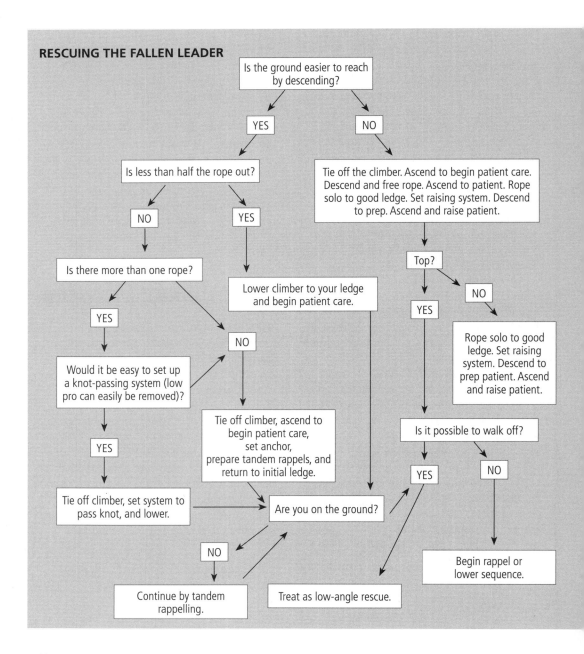

Is the ground easier to reach by descending?

- **YES**
  - **Is less than half the rope out?**
    - **NO**
      - **Is there more than one rope?**
        - **YES**
          - **Would it be easy to set up a knot-passing system (low pro can easily be removed)?**
            - **YES**
              - **Tie off climber, set system to pass knot, and lower.**
        - **NO**
          - **Tie off climber, ascend to begin patient care, set anchor, prepare tandem rappels, and return to initial ledge.**
    - **YES**
      - **Lower climber to your ledge and begin patient care.**
- **NO**
  - **Tie off the climber. Ascend to begin patient care. Descend and free rope. Ascend to patient. Rope solo to good ledge. Set raising system. Descend to prep. Ascend and raise patient.**
    - **Top?**
      - **YES**
      - **NO**
        - **Rope solo to good ledge. Set raising system. Descend to prep patient. Ascend and raise patient.**
          - **Is it possible to walk off?**
            - **YES**
            - **NO**
              - **Begin rappel or lower sequence.**

Are you on the ground?
- **NO**
  - **Continue by tandem rappelling.**

Treat as low-angle rescue.

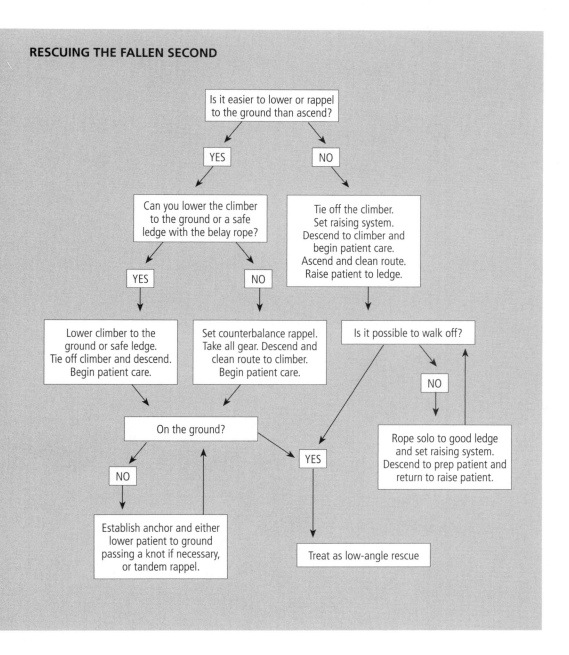

Is it easier to lower or rappel to the ground than ascend?

YES → Can you lower the climber to the ground or a safe ledge with the belay rope?

NO → Tie off the climber. Set raising system. Descend to climber and begin patient care. Ascend and clean route. Raise patient to ledge.

YES → Lower climber to the ground or safe ledge. Tie off climber and descend. Begin patient care.

NO → Set counterbalance rappel. Take all gear. Descend and clean route to climber. Begin patient care.

Is it possible to walk off?

NO → Rope solo to good ledge and set raising system. Descend to prep patient and return to raise patient.

On the ground?

NO → Establish anchor and either lower patient to ground passing a knot if necessary, or tandem rappel.

YES → Treat as low-angle rescue

CHAPTER 2

The Munter-mule-overhand, a fundamental rescue knot

Rescue Knots

In this chapter we focus on tips and tricks for tying a few knots commonly used for rescue (chosen in part for their simplicity and their familiarity to many people). There are of course plenty of other acceptable knots. Check out appendix E for additional knot references.

It is important to become proficient and confident with these ties so that when trouble hits you can concentrate on the epic at hand, not whether you tied your knot correctly. Practice tying these knots in both hands as well as in the dark. This may sound silly now, but it won't the first time you're rigging a system high on a cliff as night falls around you.

KNOT TERMINOLOGY

BIGHTS AND LOOPS

A *bight* is like a half circle; there is an obvious curve in the rope, but the rope strands do not cross one another. (See fig 2-1).

A *loop* is like a full circle; the rope strands *do* cross and the circle is closed. It can be tied anywhere along the rope. When a loop is in your palm, at the spot where the strands cross, one strand is

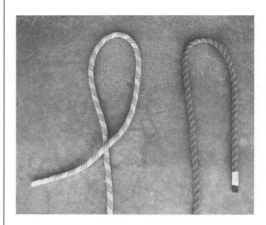

Fig. 2-1. A loop (left) crosses itself while a bight (right) remains open.

considered the bottom strand (against your hand), and the other is the top strand (closer to your eyes).

WORKING END, STANDING END

When tying a knot, the *working end* is the side of the rope that leads to the active climber or is the section of rope used to tie the knot. The *standing end* is the side of the rope leading to the anchor, the inactive climber, or is simply the end that runs into your rope bag.

LOAD STRAND, BRAKE STRAND

After a knot is tied, the *load strand* refers to whichever strand of rope is actively holding the load (e.g., the climber). In the case of a belay setup, the *brake strand* refers to the side of rope breaking a climber's fall and/or the strand that will be fed through a belay device to lower a climber. These terms are often used instead of working end and standing end, though for ease of explanation we use both sets of terms.

KNOT COMBINATIONS

Munter-mule-overhand (MMO). The Munter-mule-overhand is a *releasable hitch* whose application is introduced in chapter 3, Escaping a Belay. The mule hitch must always be backed up, either with an overhand knot or with a carabiner; see instructions later in this chapter for tying both the Munter and the mule. When we refer to the setup repeatedly, we simply use the abbreviation MMO.

Prusik-Munter-mule-overhand (PMMO). This is a series of hitches tied with a corde-lette: a Prusik hitch tied with one end (and attached to the rope) and an MMO tied with the other. Its application is explained in chapter 3, Escaping a Belay. Like the MMO, it is referred to throughout the book; we abbreviate it as PMMO. (See instructions later in this chapter for tying each hitch in this series.)

KNOT FAMILIES: LOOPS, BENDS, AND HITCHES

LOOPS

Loops form a continuous circle and can be tied anywhere along a rope. Changing the size of a loop is simple—just loosen the knot (no need to undo it!) then thread through the appropriate amount of rope to achieve the desired size. Knots that form loops discussed in this book include the figure eight on a bight, overhand on a bight, and the butterfly.

BENDS

As the saying goes, "bends join ends." Examples of *bends* discussed in this book include the water knot, Flemish bend (aka figure eight bend), and the double fisherman's. The tails of the knot exit in opposite directions. These bends are generally favored for ease of tying and security once tied.

HITCHES

Hitches have to be tied around something in order to maintain their form. Hitches have a huge role in rescue and include friction hitches used for ascending and descending lines. Any material (i.e., webbing, cord) routinely used as a friction hitch should be inspected frequently for wear due to the greater amount of abrasion it receives. Hitches covered include the clove, Munter, mule, klemheist, autoblock, Penberthy, Bachmann, mariner's, Garda, and the Prusik.

KNOT TYING AND TIPS

DRESSING THE KNOT

A well-dressed knot is a correctly tied knot; it does not have any kinks or loose or unnecessarily twisted portions. It has also been "set" or snugged down with a good tug prior to loading. (See fig. 2-2.) Dressing a

Fig. 2-2. Dressed knot. Left: Dressed and set figure eight on a bight. Right: Knot is not dressed.

knot serves a variety of purposes: it makes the knot much easier to visually inspect and it eliminates the potential for loose bits to get snagged, which might loosen or undo the knot. Some argue that undressed kinked portions add unnecessary turns, thereby reducing the knot's efficiency (i.e., strength); others say this loss of strength is minimal, and indeed an undressed figure eight is still incredibly strong. Friction hitches in particular do not grip the rope correctly unless properly dressed. *Dressed knots* are also generally easier to untie.

TAILS AND BACKUP KNOTS

Long tails and backup knots are used by many climbers to protect a knot's tail from slipping through and untying the knot as the knot is loaded and unloaded (a process known as *cyclical loading*). There is some value in using long tails and backups, but there are also some common misconceptions about them.

A rough guideline is that knot tails should be twice the length of the original knot. Having a few extra inches of tail also acts as a safeguard should your knot get snagged, and thereby inadvertently loosened.

A few climbing knots, such as many bowline variations, can loosen due to the effects of cyclical loading. These should be tied with backup knots. Slippery hitches like the mule also warrant a backup knot. The name of these knots says it all; they like to slip.

Water knots are subject to cyclical loading, but it takes such a high number of pulls for the tails to slip though the knot that it is not necessary to tie water knots with backup knots; long tails are adequate. It is a very good idea to periodically retie or, at the very least, inspect anything tied with a water knot.

Important note: To avoid redundancy, all knot-tying descriptions assume that readers will dress each knot and check that each knot is tied with adequate tail length.

WHICH KNOT TO USE?

Hopefully a variety of factors (and not just rote memorization) play into your decision of what knot to use when and where. Here are some considerations to help you choose the best knot depending upon the circumstances.

Strength. Is the knot strong enough for the job? Will it retain its strength despite the anticipated direction of pull? For example, a butterfly knot would be a better choice for three-way loading than an overhand on a bight.

Familiarity with the knot/ease of tying. This is a rescue—no time for mistakes or fiddling with difficult knots. For example, although slightly weaker than a figure eight, a bowline is typically much quicker to tie off around a tree (and is more easily adjustable) than retracing a figure eight follow-through.

Versatility. Is the knot easily convertible into a different knot or can it be used for a variety of purposes? Do you need versatility?

Compactness. Most likely you will not have an unlimited amount of rope at your disposal; the amount of rope that knots consume varies. For example, a figure eight on a bight consumes twice as much rope as a single bowline backed up with a Yosemite finish.

Ease of untying. You may not want to waste precious time untying stubborn knots. Is the knot easy to untie and adjust once it has been weighted?

KNOTS

WATER KNOT (AKA OVERHAND BEND, RING BEND)

The water knot (fig. 2-3) is typically used to connect two pieces of webbing together to create an extension or to tie a runner. As with any bend, the two ends feed out from opposite sides of the knot. If the two ends exit the knot on the same side, you have retraced your way to an overhand on a bight. Make sure to set the

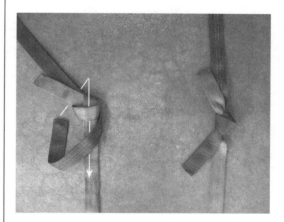

Fig. 2-3. Water knot. The dark webbing retraces the overhand knot tied on the light webbing. The tails exit from opposite sides.

knot tightly before loading; the tails have been known to slip under load when not properly set.

1. Tie an overhand knot 2 to 3 inches away from the end of a piece of webbing.
2. Bring the other end of webbing up to the knot's tail and retrace the overhand knot beginning from the tail side. The knot should be completed with the two ends exiting on opposite sides.

Fig. 2-4. Figure eight on a bight. A figure eight on a bight looks exactly like a figure eight follow-through. The difference is that with a figure eight on a bight you cannot tie the loop through something (like a belay loop) without a carabiner, while because of the retrace step in a figure eight follow-through you can.

FIGURE EIGHT AND FIGURE EIGHT ON A BIGHT

Considering that these are beginning climbing knots, their tying instructions have not been included. The figure eight and figure eight on a bight (fig. 2-4) certainly consume more rope than other knots, but they are also easier to undo than an overhand on a bight, for example; a consideration for heavy rescue loads. All members of the figure eight family can also be tied in webbing (it makes for a much stronger knot than an overhand; however, figure eights tied in webbing can be very difficult to untie).

A variation of the figure eight on a bight is a *figure nine*. A figure nine simply employs another wrap around the middle of the eight before inserting through the final loop. A figure nine, although messy looking, creates a bulkier knot, which can make skinnier cord that has been holding heavy loads (as in a rescue) easier to untie. Tests show the figure nine to be stronger than the figure eight.

FLEMISH BEND (AKA FIGURE EIGHT BEND)

A Flemish bend (fig. 2-5) is used almost exclusively with cord and rope, although it can certainly be tied with webbing (a bit messy and difficult to dress). As with a water knot, the tails exit the knot in opposite directions. This is what distinguishes a Flemish bend from a figure eight on a bight or a figure eight follow-through. The Flemish bend is much easier to tie, adjust, and untie after being loaded than a double

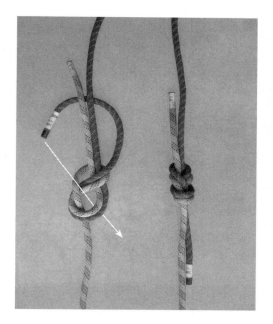

Fig. 2-6. Double fisherman's. The light cord circles twice around the dark cord forming an X. The tail then slides under and out through the X (indicated by the arrow.) The two knots are pulled tight so that the two Xs are snug against each other.

Fig. 2-5. Flemish bend. The dark rope retraces the simple figure eight tied on the light rope. The tails exit in opposite directions.

fisherman's, and it is a good knot for creating a quick, improvisational cordelette loop. Although a bit bulkier than an overhand knot (aka "eurodeath knot"), the Flemish bend is also good for linking two rappel ropes together since it is easy to tie and untie, strong, and has a relatively narrow profile.

1. Tie a figure eight 2 to 3 inches away from the end of a piece of cord or rope.
2. Retrace the figure eight with another strand of rope, taking care to initiate the retracing from the knot's tail, ensuring that the tails will exit in opposite directions.

DOUBLE FISHERMAN'S

The double fisherman's is popular for creating rescue loops (see chapter 1, "Equipment"). It also can be tied on the end of a rope as a stopper knot to avoid rappelling off the end of the rope or allowing the end of a rope to slip through a device when belaying or lowering. Some climbers also use this knot for linking two rappel ropes together. When used as a bend, a double fisherman's is tied on either side of the line and pulled together as shown in fig. 2-6.

1. Take one end of the rope and wrap it around the other rope (or the end

of the same rope) in two complete circles. The first circle should be made moving away from you while the second circle comes back towards you, creating an X where the two circles cross.

2. Find the X, created by rope crossing over itself, and thread the tail under and through that X, exiting in line with the strand of rope you have tied your knot around. The tail should exit under and through the x away from you.

When joining two ropes together (or creating a loop out of cord), tie the same knot with the other tail. Bring the two knots snug up against each other and rotate until the two Xs are lined up. Cinch down to set.

HITCHES

MUNTER HITCH

The Munter hitch is a versatile and quick hitch that can be used for lowering or belaying, as well as for rappelling in place of a belay device. The Munter is unique in that it has two positions (lowering and taking in slack) and depending on how the climber is weighting the rope (being lowered or climbing), the hitch will need to rotate between

Fig. 2-7. Munter hitch. Top: Step 1. Bottom: Step 2. Step 3 is to clip the carabiner around the two strands of rope directly above the carabiner as indicated by the arrow.

Fig. 2-8. Building a Munter on a carabiner. Steps 2 and 3: Bring a bight of rope from behind the loaded strand and clip the bight into the carabiner as shown in photostrands of rope directly above the carabiner as indicated by the arrow.

Fig. 2-9. Loaded Munter. Note how the hitch rotates around the carabiner depending upon how the hitch is being used. Left: Munter is rotated for lowering. Right: Munter is rotated for taking in slack.

those two positions. Although the hitch's orientation can change, the load strand should be located on the spine side. Using a Munter does generate a large amount of friction but the friction of rope on rope is not of concern because the sections of rope rubbing against each other are constantly changing.

1. Place a loop of rope flat in your hand, the circle oriented away from you as shown in fig. 2-7.
2. Fold the loop over itself, toward you. The (formerly) top strand should now be sandwiched between two sections of the bottom strand.
3. Clip a carabiner around the two stacked strands.

Another handy way to tie a Munter is to build it directly on the carabiner; this is also an easy way to ensure that the load strand is tied on the spine side:

1. Clip a bight of rope in to a locking carabiner with the gate screwing downward.
2. Grab the unweighted strand of rope from behind the loaded strand and bring it around in front of the load strand.
3. Clip a bight of the unweighted strand in to the carabiner (fig. 2-8). You do not need to change your hand position or change the unloaded strand's orientation (e.g., don't twist it, etc.) to do this.
4. Make sure to set the knot in the correct position (so that the load strand is in fact loaded) before the climber weights the rope (see fig. 2-9).

MULE HITCH

The mule hitch allows a belay to be tied off, giving the belayer the ability to remove her brake hand from the rope and attain the hands-free position. Many knots work okay for this purpose, but the mule hitch is a reliable slippery hitch that is relatively easy to remove after loading. It combines well with a Munter, making it the hitch of choice, and is an important component of rope rescue.

Because it is a slippery hitch, the mule is always backed up. An easy and reliable backup is an overhand on a bight tied around the load strand with the working end. Another option, which uses much less rope, is to clip the loop (coming off the mule hitch) with a carabiner to the load strand (fig. 7-4 in chapter 7 shows this backup method).

TYING OFF A MUNTER BELAY WITH A MULE HITCH

1. While maintaining a safe belay, create a loop with the brake strand. The portion of the brake strand closest to the Munter must be stacked between the load strand and the standing end of the brake strand (the circle in fig. 2-10).
2. Make a bight of rope in the standing end of the brake strand ("2A" in fig. 2-10), and push it through the loop you just created, making sure to travel in a direction that wraps the brake strand in a half circle around the load strand ("2B" in fig. 2-11).
3. Cinch the mule hitch down (fig. 2-12).
4. Tie a backup knot as close to the

TYING OFF A MUNTER BELAY WITH A MULE HITCH

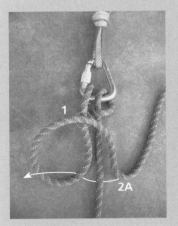

Fig. 2-10. Step 1 and beginning of step 2.

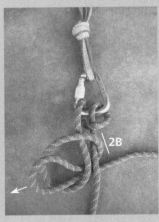

Fig. 2-11. Step 2: the brake strand makes a half circle around the load strand.

Fig. 2-12. Step 3.

Fig. 2-13. Step 4; arrow indicates the path for tying an overhand.

Fig. 2-14. Completed mule hitch with an overhand back-up tying off a Munter belay.

TYING A MULE HITCH ON A BELAY DEVICE

Fig. 2-15. Step 1: Note the sharp kink in the belay strand (1A).

Fig. 2-16. Step 2.

Fig. 2-17. Step 3.

Fig. 2-18. Completed mule hitch with an overhand backup tying off an ATC belay.

mule hitch as possible (fig. 2-13). A good backup knot is an overhand on a bight tied around the load strand with the mule tail. *Note:* To keep the mule and the backup knot as close to the Munter as possible, work on a plane perpendicular to the rope rather than pulling and tightening up and away from the Munter (see fig. 2-18, which shows the same tie-off with a belay device). Figure 2-14 shows a completed Munter-mule-overhand (MMO).

TYING A MULE HITCH ON A BELAY DEVICE

1. Using your fingers to maintain the rope's braking position (that sharp kink in the belay strand as it exits the belay device; "1A" in fig. 2-15), pass a bight of rope through the open space of the carabiner (fig. 2-15).
2. Twist that bight into a loop, taking care to stack the section of brake strand closest to the ATC between the standing end and the loaded climbing rope (dashed circle in fig. 2-16); pull more slack through if you need it.
3 and 4. Pick up at step 3 of tying off a Munter with a mule (fig. 2-17 and 2-18). Pull any slack out on a plane perpendicular to the rope and belay device (see arrow in fig. 2-17). This helps keep the backup knot close to the mule.

To release the mule, just work your way backward, but be careful! If using a belay device, make sure to maintain that sharp

kink in the brake strand next to the device (see "1A" in fig. 2-15 and step 1 of tying a mule on a belay device) as you return the brake strand to its standard belaying position. (If the kink is not maintained you could lose belaying control as you undo the mule.) Warn your climber that he might feel a little pop as the mule is released.

CLOVE HITCH

The clove hitch is an effective knot for securing a line, weighted or unweighted, into a carabiner. Instead of using *daisy chains,* many climbers (especially alpinists, in their effort to climb fast and light) tie in to belay anchors with clove hitches, which are easy to adjust and untie. Unlike some other hitches, the clove hitch has the advantage of holding tight when just one strand is weighted. If weighted and unweighted repeatedly, the clove hitch can loosen and if not properly tightened it may creep up and potentially open the gate of a nonlocking carabiner. For this reason it is recommended to not leave clove hitches unattended and to use a locking carabiner.

As with the Munter, you should ideally tie this hitch so that the load strand is on the carabiner's spine side. Weighting a carabiner's gate axis can decrease the carabiner's strength considerably.

1. Take a bight of rope in either hand, leaving only a few inches of space between the two bights.
2. Rotate both bights half a circle in the same direction to create two loops.
3. Bring the two loops together,

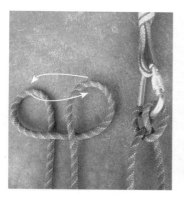  

Fig. 2-19. Clove hitch. Left: Step 3; bring the loop on the left in front of the loop on the right. Right: Step 4; completed clove hitch clipped through the anchor's master point.

Fig. 2-20. Building a clove hitch on a carabiner. Bring a bight of rope from behind the load strand; create a loop by turning the bight in a half circle back toward the carabiner's spine, and then drop that loop into the carabiner. Note how the loop on the left is closed off on the opposite side of the rope than the loop on the right.

Fig. 2-21. Building a clove hitch on a carabiner. Clip the loop through the carabiner to complete the clove hitch.

making sure to sandwich the two longer strands (that dangle down) together (fig. 2-19).

4. Clip a carabiner through the two loops.

The ability to build a clove hitch on a carabiner is a useful skill for a variety of situations. If you are belaying your follower on a Munter, the Munter can quickly be switched to a clove hitch (assuming your climber is in a safe, stable position). Additionally, tying a clove hitch directly on the anchor ensures that the load strand will be on the spine side of the carabiner. See figs. 2-20 and 2-21.

FRICTION HITCHES

Friction hitches are vital rescue knots used for ascending, descending, and holding loads at specific spots on a rope. The hitch can slide along the line but once weighted will grip the rope at that spot and hold its position on the line.

It is very important to always (yes, *always*) test your friction hitch prior to loading it for real to ensure that it grips and slides when necessary. Every rope is a little different. Newer ropes can be more slippery than older ones and so might need another wrap thrown on to make sure the hitch grabs. The number of wraps needed for any friction hitch also depends on the comparative diameter of the rope and the cord being used; the larger the difference the fewer the wraps. You may also find yourself adjusting the number of wraps if ropes are wet or snowy or if you are dealing with a large load. Hanging midair, slowly slipping, is not the place to realize you could have used another wrap in your friction hitch. *HMPE* materials (like Dyneema and Spectra sewn runners) are not recommended for friction hitches because of their low melting point and slippery texture.

PRUSIK HITCH

The Prusik hitch provides the tightest grip on the rope of all friction hitches. But that also creates its biggest downfall; it can be difficult to untie or slide after holding a large load. With the exception of laid ropes, which are rarely used by modern climbers, another advantage is that a Prusik does a great job holding a load in any direction. The two-wrap Prusik is adequate for many things but a Prusik hitch with three wraps (called an "improved Prusik hitch" by some) is recommended for rescue applications; the extra wrap creates more surface area for grabbing the rope. Throughout this book we simply use "Prusik hitch" to mean a three-wrap Prusik. Cord is the preferred material for tying Prusiks; however, nylon webbing can be used. With webbing you should use more wraps, and Prusiks tied in webbing are much more difficult to release once weighted.

1. Make a rescue loop with a 4-foot piece of 7-millimeter cord, connecting the two ends with a double fisherman's or a Flemish bend.
2. Hold one side of the loop in either hand, placing the knot in the other hand, and stretch the loop out to full length (fig. 2-22, left).
3. Bring your hands together around the rope, passing the knot through the inside of the loop as if you were putting on a luggage tag (fig. 2-22, right).
4. Repeat this process (for a total of three times), making sure to wrap in the same direction and always wrapping through the middle of the loop (fig. 2-22, right).
5. Move your hand just a few inches off the knot to either side.
6. Pull the loop directly away from the rope, allowing the wraps to cinch down (fig. 2-23, left).
7. In order to properly dress the Prusik, you must sort the wraps over one another until there are no crisscrosses and they are all lying flat, tight in line on the rope (fig. 2-23, right). Picture a well-dressed Prusik as four straight teeth in the center with a large lower lip running in an uninterrupted crescent shape from left to right on the outside. Once the Prusik is loaded and bites down, these loops will shift somewhat. Should you need to change the Prusik's position on the line, unweight it, then loosen up the lower lip (or "brake bar") with your thumb. Now slide the Prusik to the desired new spot on the rope and weight as needed.

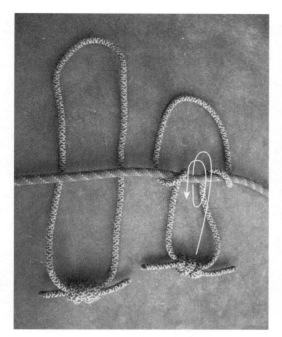 

*Fig. 2-22. Three-wrap Prusik. Left: Step 2.
Right: Steps 3 and 4.*

*Fig. 2-23. Three-wrap Prusik. Left: Steps 5 and 6.
Right: Step 7; completed and dressed Prusik.*

To quickly remove the Prusik, grab the lower lip and pull straight out, away from the rope to which it is hitched.

It is important to emphasize with climbers new to friction hitches that you should not grab them; you should push them. With a Prusik, push it with your thumb from either above or below depending on your direction of travel. Grabbing the Prusik or wrapping your hand over it does not allow it to grip the rope. The best way to let the Prusik grip is to let go of it. In a panic a climber may forget to let go of the Prusik, his hand inadvertently keeping the Prusik open and causing him to slide down the line.

AUTOBLOCK HITCH

The autoblock is a releasable hitch that is quite similar to the Prusik both in form and function. It is a bit quicker to tie than a Prusik and is easier to remove, especially when weighted, but it does not grip as quickly or as firmly as a Prusik. Autoblocks should be used with caution in snowy conditions such as crevasse rescue. Compared to a Prusik it is easier for snow to get in between the looser wraps on an autoblock, loosening

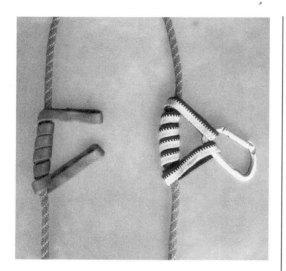

Fig. 2-24. Autoblock. Left: Step 2. Right: Step 3; completed autoblock.

Fig. 2-25. Tying an autoblock with a Penberthy

their grip on the rope and thereby decreasing the hitch's holding power.

1. Make a rescue loop with a 4-foot piece of 7-millimeter cord (or $^9/_{16}$-inch webbing), connecting the two ends with a double fisherman's, a Flemish bend, or a water knot.
2. Wrap the loop four to six times (depending on diameter of lines, conditions, and length of the loop) around the rope (fig. 2-24, left).
3. Bring the two ends together and clip a carabiner through both ends (fig. 2-24, right).

To undo the autoblock, simply unclip one side of the loop from the carabiner and unwind.

An autoblock can also be tied using a strand of cord tied off with two overhand knots on either end. This single-strand version is called a *Penberthy.* Follow the same steps as described for tying an autoblock. Clip the carabiner through the two loops created by the overhand knots. See fig. 2-25. This is a great hitch for a third-hand *rappel backup,* discussed in chapter 4.

KLEMHEIST

The klemheist is almost identical to the autoblock but is generally constructed with fewer wraps and a different final step. Like the autoblock, the klemheist is much easier to release under load compared to a Prusik. According to tests, klemheists also have better gripping power than autoblocks. Unlike the other friction hitches already introduced, the klemheist will grab best in one direction, dictated by how it is tied.

1. Make a rescue loop with a 4-foot piece of 7-millimeter cord (or ⁹/₁₆-inch webbing), connecting the two ends with a double fisherman's, a Flemish bend, or a water knot.

2. Just like an autoblock, wrap the runner four to six times (depending on diameter of lines, conditions, and length of the loop) around the load strand. But make sure to leave more tail on the bottom portion of the runner.

3. Instead of simply bringing the two end bights together, feed the bottom end bight up through the top end bight (fig. 2-26, left).

4. Pull all the slack through and clip a carabiner into the bottom end bight (fig. 2-26, right). The klemheist will grip best when the bottom end bight is pulled downward.

Fig. 2-26. Klemheist. Left: Step 2, with Step 3 shown by an arrow. Right: Step 4; completed klemheist.

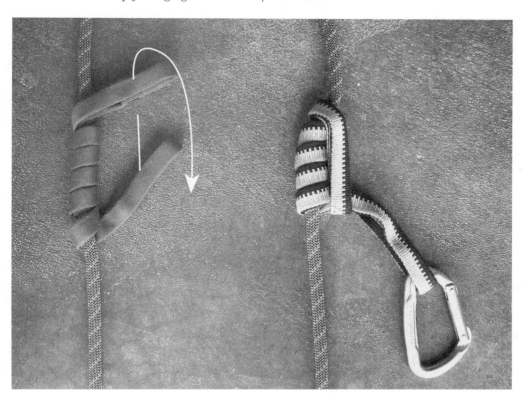

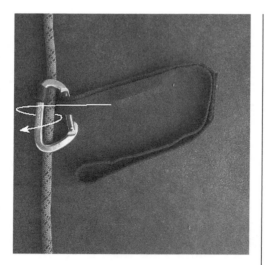

Fig. 2-27. Bachmann. Steps 1 and 2. Note the runner clipped through the carabiner and the arrow indicating the direction in which the runner should be wrapped.

BACHMANN

The Bachmann is another knot that can be used for ascension, with the advantage of the carabiner acting as a handle that can slide up and down the line. The Bachmann can be tied with either cord or webbing. Like the klemheist, the Bachmann catches best in one direction.

1. Clip a carabiner through the end of a runner.
2. Lay the carabiner up against the rope. Wrap the runner around the rope and the spine of the carabiner three to four times, moving down the carabiner's spine as you wrap but keeping the webbing or cord neat (fig. 2-27). The actual number of wraps will depend upon the diameters of your cord or runner and of the rope.
3. Finish the hitch off by wrapping the runner through the carabiner one last time, but not around the rope. The runner exits directly off the carabiner (fig. 2-28).
4. Clip in to the runner. The carabiner acts as a handle to slide the hitch along the line but is not load bearing.

GARDA HITCH

The Garda hitch is a type of friction hitch tied with just the climbing rope and two carabiners. The rope can move one way

Fig. 2-28. Bachmann. Step 3: Completed knot. Note how the runner exits directly off the carabiner, not off the rope.

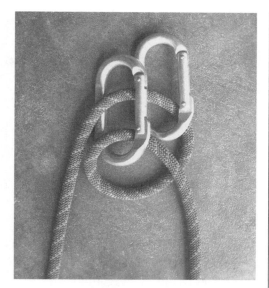

Fig. 2-29. Garda. The left rope strand will hold the load while the right strand can be pulled through the carabiners.

through the carabiners; it is blocked from moving the other way. The Garda, when combined with an additional friction hitch, provides another way of ascending a line (see chapter 5, Ascending). The Garda can also be incorporated into a simple raising system, although it has the disadvantage of not being reversible or easily releasable under a load. The Garda works best with carabiners of the same size. If tied with nonlocking carabiners the Garda should be attended to avoid the rope creeping up and slipping through a gate after repeated loading and unloading.

1. Clip a bight of rope through two carabiners.

2. Make a loop on one side of the rope.

3. Clip the loop into the carabiner farthest from the loop. The rope will be pulled freely through this side. The side that holds the load *does not* receive the additional loop of rope and is the side of rope that you do not want slipping (e.g., your load if you are hauling, or the remaining portion of line you have yet to ascend). See fig. 2-29.

MARINER'S HITCH

The *mariner's hitch* is a releasable hitch used to make a system reversible, just like the Munter-mule combination. The mariner's is attached to the anchor on one end, and on the other end is some sort of friction device or knot in the climbing rope. The mariner's can transfer a load (lowering it a short distance), but should not be released and then relied upon as a belay, whereas the Munter-mule setup can be. Care should be taken to carefully tie (or clip) off the mariner's so it does not slip over time. Both cord and webbing are acceptable materials for tying the mariner's (although HMPE sewn runners are not recommended).

1. Attach a cordalette (or runner) to the climbing rope with a friction hitch or to a knot on the rope.

2. Bring the cordalette back up to a locking carabiner located on either the anchor's master point (MP) or shelf. Wrap the cordalette around the carabiner. (An alternative is to thread

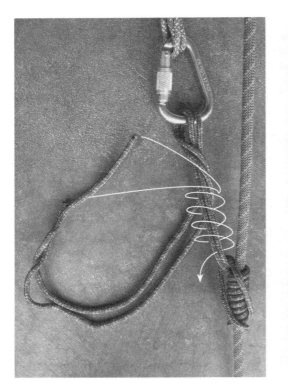

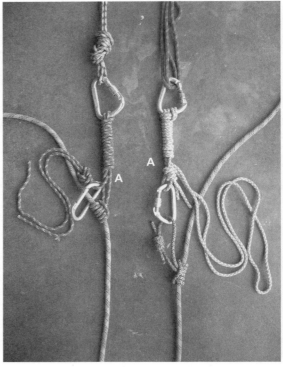

Fig. 2-30. Mariner's hitch. Steps 1 and 2: The cord is attached to the rope with a klemheist and goes back up to a carabiner, around which the cord is wrapped. Step 3: Loop the cord around its two strands at least five times, as indicated by the arrow.

Fig. 2-31. Mariner's hitch. Left: Completed knot. Note how the tail is threaded through the two strands of the cord ("A"), with the tail clipped off to the climbing rope with a carabiner (Step 4). Right: Munter-mariner's. The setup is shown tied with a rescue loop and a separate piece of cord versus the single continuous strand in the left example.

a Munter hitch around the carabiner, creating a Munter-mariner's combination; see fig. 2-31.)

3. Wrap the cordalette back around itself (between the climbing rope and the carabiner) at least five times (fig. 2-30).

4. Slip the end of the cordalette through the two strands of the cordalette you have just been wrapping. To keep the mariner's from coming undone, tie the mariner's tail unto a loop and bight of the mariner's and clip the loop around the climbing rope with a carabiner (fig. 2-31).

To release the mariner's, slowly undo the wraps and allow slack to slowly feed through the system until the load is transferred back to the climbing rope.

If you have a long enough section of cord you can tie a mariner's with one piece of material. Double the material up (creating a large bight) so you have two strands. Tie a friction hitch at the top of the bight and use the tails to tie a mariner's hitch back at the anchor. Figs. 2-30 and 2-31 (left) show this method.

A climber's normal gear rack generally contains all the gear necessary for a rescue.

ROPE MANAGEMENT

Good rope management becomes especially crucial in rescue. As you bring multiple strands back to the anchor make sure they are attached in an order and place on the anchor that leaves them easily accessible—not caught up by the weight of other ropes or gear, and free of getting tangled.

TABLE 2.1 SUMMARY OF RESCUE HITCHES

Hitch	Use	Pros	Cons
autoblock	▪ Ascending and descending a line ▪ Grabbing the rope at a fixed point on the line ▪ Somewhat releasable hitch	▪ Very quick to tie ▪ Moves up and down the line with greater ease than a Prusik ▪ Can be loaded in either direction ▪ Relatively easy to release under load	▪ Weakest gripping strength of presented friction hitches ▪ Sometimes slow to grab; needs to be set carefully ▪ Use with caution in snowy conditions ▪ Abrupt load release
Bachmann	▪ Ascending and descending a line ▪ Grabbing the rope at a fixed point on the line	▪ Good grip strength especially in one direction ▪ Carabiner can be used as a handle to slide the hitch	▪ Weighting the carabiner handle can also cause the hitch to slip ▪ Less grip than a Prusik ▪ Need webbing or cord and a carabiner to construct
Garda	▪ Works like a ratcheting Prusik in a raising system ▪ Can be used for ascending	▪ Easy hitch to tie with practice ▪ Requires minimal gear (two carabiners) ▪ Has a very strong grip; creates a lot of friction	▪ Not releasable under load ▪ Can be difficult to pull rope through due to high amount of friction
klemheist	▪ Ascending and descending a line ▪ Grabbing the rope at a fixed point on the line	▪ Moves up and down the line with greater ease than a Prusik ▪ Gripping strength is high but not as strong as a Prusik ▪ Sometimes able to release under load	▪ Grips best only in one direction ▪ Use caution in snowy conditions
mariner's	▪ Load releasing hitch for short load release transitions like escaping a belay or passing a knot	▪ Fast and easy to tie ▪ Can be effectively tied with both webbing and cord ▪ Lots of friction for controlling heavy loads	▪ Must be carefully clipped off to stay secure ▪ Uses a lot of material to tie ▪ Can only let out loads; can't belay loads in
mule	▪ Releasable tie-off for a belay	▪ Releasable under load	▪ Easily releasable; must be backed up
Munter	▪ Belaying climber in and out ▪ Rappelling	▪ Can belay rope in and out ▪ Lots of friction for controlling heavy loads ▪ Easy way to improvise a rappel	▪ Can put twists in rope, especially if used repeatedly
Prusik	▪ Ascending and descending a line ▪ Grabbing the rope at a fixed point on the line	▪ Can handle the weight of very large loads without slipping ▪ Can be loaded in either direction	▪ Once weighted, does not slide up and down the line as easily as other friction hitches ▪ Very difficult to release under load

CHAPTER 3

How many of your climbing partners are confident and competent at escaping a belay?

Escaping a Belay

The *belay escape* is a fundamental skill necessary for the majority of rescues ranging from the simple to the serious; in order to effect a rescue, a rescuer must be freed from the responsibilities of belaying. It is also a good starting point for talking about rescue systems. We use the process of escaping a belay to introduce a number of skills.

Sometimes it is possible to move into a lowering or raising sequence before completing all steps of a belay escape. It is important to know the complete system, however, before combining systems or skipping steps.

Throughout the belay escape the climber's position on the rope is maintained. The end result is a system that is releasable under load and still useable in further steps as a belay. Returning to belay mode is often a necessity once you have formulated a plan; maybe your partner needs to be lowered or, after assistance, is able to continue climbing. Either of these steps (as well as raising

and counterbalance rappelling) require that the system be releasable.

WHEN BELAYING OFF YOUR BODY

Below we describe two ways of escaping a belay if you are belaying a leader off your body with an ATC (or any tubular belay device). In subsequent sections we then cover escaping a belay when belaying directly off the anchor and when using a *redirectional piece* off the anchor.

ESCAPING A BELAY: STANDARD SEQUENCE

1. Get hands-free: Tie a mule hitch and an overhand backup on the load strand between your ATC and the climber (fig. 3-1); or, wrap the load strand around your leg multiple times to maintain the brake on the belay (these are called *"leg wraps"*;

take great care when doing your leg wraps—you do not want to introduce excess slack into the system). When tying the mule-overhand, pay special attention to maintaining a good pinch on the brake strand as you negotiate the bight of rope through the ATC; transfer your brake hand to the other side of the belay carabiner and keep the brake locked off while tying the mule-overhand. Although you are not yet out of the belay setup, once the mule-overhand is tied your hands are relieved of belay duty (you are "hands-free"), enabling you to use your hands for other tasks while your partner is securely held by the mule hitch (or the leg wraps).

2. Using a Flemish bend, tie a long cordelette into a loop.

3. Using this loop, tie a Prusik hitch onto the load strand of the climbing rope (fig. 3-2); keep the loop's knot close to the Prusik hitch. (This is the Prusik part of tying a PMMO.)

4. Next, reach back to the anchor and clip a locking pearabiner through the master point or shelf with the pearabiner's gate oriented down and out (fig. 3-2).

5. Using the long strands dangling from the cordelette, tie a Munter onto the pearabiner you just added to the anchor (this is the Munter-mule-over-hand part of tying a PMMO). Pull in all the slack and then reset the Munter into the lowering position by pulling on the load strands of the cordelette so that the Munter rotates, and tie a mule hitch with an over-hand backup (fig. 3-2).

6. Push the Prusik hitch along the rope toward the climber until the slack between the Prusik and the MMO is taken up (fig. 3-3). Be careful to not push the Prusik too far out of reach. If there is still excess slack in the cordelette between the two knots, go back up to the Munter-mule, undo the mule, and take in the excess slack using the Munter.

7. Carefully undo the mule-overhand on your ATC and let slack through the ATC, transferring the climber's weight onto the cordelette—you should not have to lower the climber much (fig. 3-3).

8. Reach back to the anchor and clip another locking carabiner through either the MP or the shelf, oriented down and out (fig. 3-4).

9. Bring the brake strand of the climbing rope back to the newly attached carabiner and tie a Munter onto the carabiner (fig. 3-4).

10. Once the Munter is tied with the brake strand of the climbing rope, bring in most of the excess rope between the Munter and your ATC, leaving just enough slack for unclipping from the device.

11. Maintaining a hand on the brake strand coming off the Munter you just tied, take your ATC off the rope.

12. Pull in all the excess slack in the climbing rope via the Munter. Finish this

ESCAPING A BELAY

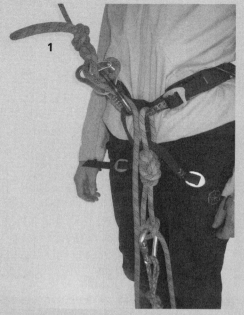

Fig. 3-1. Step 1. Note: climber is tied into the anchor with a clove hitch.

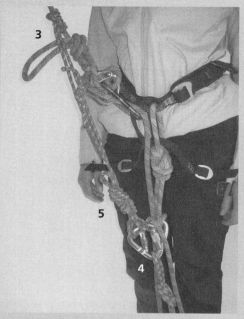

Fig. 3-2. Steps 3, 4, and 5 (Step 2 not shown.)

Fig. 3-3. Steps 6 and 7.

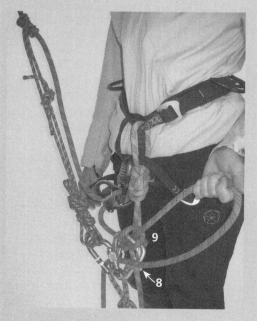

Fig. 3-4. Steps 8 and 9.

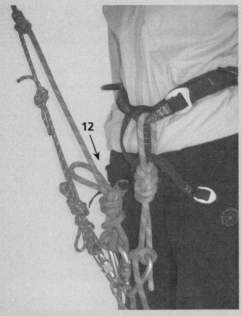

Fig. 3-5. Step 12 (steps 10 and 11 not pictured).

Fig. 3-6. Step 13.

Fig. 3-7. Completed.

step by tying a mule hitch, snug against the Munter, and an overhand backup (fig. 3-5).

13. Release the mule-overhand tied with the cordelette and use the munter to transfer the weight from the cordelette onto the climbing rope (fig. 3-6). Once the weight is fully on the climbing rope, detach the cordelette from the rope.

All you should be left with is an MMO tied with the climbing rope onto the anchor (fig. 3-7). Now you are ready to execute the plan for helping your partner.

ESCAPING A BELAY USING A RESCUE LOOP

This second way of escaping a belay is a great method if you are far from the anchor and/or do not have a long cordelette. This method has the advantage of only using one short rescue loop (with a Prusik hitch) and a couple of locking carabiners. It is quick and easy to adapt to many situations. Be careful to tie off the main climbing rope to the main anchor to finish this belay escape, especially if you are using a clove hitch as your personal anchor tie-in.

1. Get hands-free by tying a mule hitch and overhand backup (fig. 3-8), or do

ESCAPING A BELAY USING A RESCUE LOOP

Fig. 3-8. Step 1. (The "3" indicates the strand of rope that will be used to complete Step 3.)

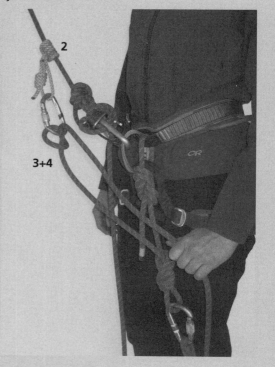

Fig. 3-9. Steps 2, 3, and 4. The mule-overhand has yet to be tied.

Fig. 3-10. Steps 5 and 6

Fig. 3-11. Step 7 completed.

Fig. 3-12. Step 8

Fig-3-13. Escaping a belay using a rescue loop, completed.

some leg wraps with the load strand; see step 1 of "Escaping a Belay: Standard Sequence," above.

2. Place a rescue loop (with a Prusik hitch) onto the load strand just above the MMO, and clip a carabiner (locking, if you have it) onto the rescue loop (fig. 3-9).

3. Reach back to your tie-in at the anchor. (This is assuming the belayer is tied in to the end of the rope and then tied in to the anchor with a figure eight on a bight or a clove hitch.) Take the free strand of your tie-in (not the strand attaching you to the anchor) and bring it forward to the carabiner clipped through the rescue loop (fig. 3-9). If you can't reach your anchor, grab your rope stack and run through that until you get to the other side of your anchor tie-in.

4. With the free strand, tie a MMO onto the rescue loop carabiner (fig. 3-9).

5. Slide the rescue loop Prusik hitch along the rope toward the climber to take out the slack (fig. 3-10).

6. Transfer the load onto the rescue loop Prusik by letting slack through your ATC (fig. 3-10).

7. Take the ATC's brake strand back to the anchor and tie a Munter onto another locking carabiner clipped directly into the anchor (fig. 3-11). Do not take your ATC off until the Munter is in place. Once the ATC is removed, bring in the excess slack and tie off the Munter with a mule-overhand.

8. Undo the mule-overhand tied on the rescue loop's carabiner. Using the Munter, slowly transfer the weight from the rescue loop onto the Munter-mule tied on the carabiner coming off the anchor (fig. 3-12). Once the weight is fully transferred, you can undo the Munter connected to the rescue loop, and remove the rescue loop from the load strand (fig. 3-13).

IMPROVISE: ESCAPING A BELAY USING A RESCUE LOOP

Here is a third belay escape method to practice. It is just another variation on the theme but is a very quick escape needing only one rescue loop, one MMO tie-off, and a few carabiners.

Follow the steps in "Escaping a Belay Using a Rescue Loop," but instead of using a Prusik hitch, use an autoblock (step 2). When tying the rope to the rescue loop carabiner in step 4, use a clove hitch or a figure eight on a bight instead of a Munter-mule. To release the load back to the main tied-off climbing rope in step 8, just pull on the top of the autoblock coils to get the autoblock to release. Be careful! The autoblock often does not release gradually. If there is a lot of slack to transfer, it might shock the system. Experienced climbers could do this while maintaining a brake hand as well.

REVIEW OF ESCAPING A BELAY

1. Get hands-free.
2. Transfer the climber's weight to the anchor.
3. Move the main belay to the anchor and tie it off.
4. Remove the cordelette or rescue loop.

WHEN BELAYING OFF THE ANCHOR

Let's first work through belaying with a Munter hitch off the anchor, and then we'll take a look at some of the other belay devices on the market.

ESCAPING A BELAY USING A MUNTER HITCH

Belaying directly off the anchor with a Munter hitch is a lightweight and simple way to belay your partner. This method makes escaping the belay unnecessary, as the belay is already on the anchor and not your harness. The disadvantages are (1) that it is not acceptable for belaying a lead climber; (2) you are belaying directly off

DO YOU NEED TO BEEF UP THE ANCHOR?

Depending on the quality of your anchor, your anticipated direction of pull, and what your next steps are, you *may* need to take the time to beef up the anchor before embarking on a rescue. Hauling, for example, exerts a much larger amount of force on an anchor compared to the forces of rappelling.

If you are simply adding to an already existing multidirectional anchor, hopefully you will be able to work the new points in with some creative sling craft. Double, triple, quadruple up slings; tie knots in runners; adjust water knots in webbing—whatever!

If you are looking at tying a lead climber off on a minimal anchor (like a single upward directional pull piece incorporated into a larger anchor), you will need to take the time to strengthen the anchor or create a new one (if you have extra gear). Most likely the leader will have all the protection pieces, though you may have slings and cordelettes. If lowering your leader is not an option (e.g., she has led past the rope's halfway point, or she has traversed or climbed over a large overhang), you may need to ascend or rope solo up to retrieve some of the pieces your leader placed lower down, to use in reinforcing the anchor. See chapter 5, Ascending.

First, take the same initial step of getting your hands free. If the anchor needs to be reinforced for an upward pull, try to change the webbing or cord in the anchor for better direction of pull. It may also be possible to reposition a piece or two for better upward pull. Caution: Do not jeopardize your security! Make sure the anchor still protects you from a fall. After you reinforce the anchor, pick up where you left off in the process of escaping the belay; your hands are already free, now it is time to escape the belay.

the anchor (only a problem if your anchor is questionable or poorly positioned); and (3) many people complain about the kinks that belaying with a Munter creates.

Follow these steps for escaping a belay using a Munter hitch:

1. Make sure the Munter is in the lowering position, with the climber weighting the rope.
2. Tie a mule hitch and backup knot against the Munter. With that simple step you have both freed your hands and escaped the belay.

ESCAPING A BELAY USING A SELF-BLOCKING BELAY DEVICE

A self-blocking belay device allows a lead climber to give her second a belay while maintaining just a light hand on the brake strand. This is extremely useful when climbing long multipitch routes. The slack generated by the follower can be pulled in through the belay device but not pulled out; when weighted, the device and carabiner lock down on the rope. This allows the belayer to use her hands for other tasks (putting on another layer, getting food and water, or reorganizing gear for the next pitch) while still giving a secure belay. *Note:* manufacturers recommend that a light brake hand should be maintained even with a self-blocking device. Examples of such devices are the Trango B-52, Kong GiGi, New Alp Plaquette, and the Petzl Reverso.

As with belaying off the anchor with a Munter, the majority of your work escaping the belay is already done. By virtue of belaying with a self-blocking belay device

Fig. 3-14. A self-blocking belay device backed up by a figure eight on a bight ("A"), clipped off to the anchor

your hands are already free and you have escaped the belay. The only step left to do is back up the system. Tie a mule-overhand or a backup knot onto the main line as a backup (fig. 3-14 shows a figure eight on a bight as the backup knot).

ESCAPING A BELAY USING LOCKING-ASSIST BELAY DEVICES

The Trango Cinch and Petzl GriGri are popular belay devices with locking-assist mechanisms and are commonly used at crags and on big walls. With these, it is pos-

Fig. 3-15. In some situations, some climbers prefer to belay through a redirectional piece off the anchor.

sible to give a lead or following climber a solid belay. (A light grip should be maintained on the brake strand at all times.) Be aware that these devices can slowly "ooze" out small amounts of slack when holding a load over a longer period of time. Therefore it is necessary to put in some sort of backup while you escape the belay. Tie a mule-overhand as you would if you were belaying with a regular device, or tie a backup knot, like a figure eight on a bight, and clip it to the anchor.

Fig. 3-16. Escaping a belay using a redirectional.
Steps 1 and 2 completed.

Fig. 3-17. Escaping a belay using a redirectional.
Step 3 completed; belayer is in the process of
completing step 4.

WHEN BELAYING USING A REDIRECTIONAL PIECE

For more comfortable positioning, a redirectional piece might be preferred to directly belaying off the anchor especially if you do not have a self-blocking belay device and do not like using a Munter (fig. 3-15). Using a redirectional piece multiplies forces on the anchor (a 2:1 ratio of *force* is created) versus belaying directly off the anchor, so make sure the anchor and rock quality are bomber.

1. Get hands-free (fig. 3-16); see step 1 of "Escaping a Belay: Standard Sequence."
2. The PMMO step: Using a cordelette, set a Prusik on the load strand (leading to the climber). Tie a MMO with the cordelette onto a new locking carabiner clipped into the anchor's master point or shelf (2 on fig. 3-16).
3. Lower the climber's weight onto the Prusik and tie a MMO with the

climbing rope to a locking carabiner on the MP (fig. 3-17). Simply let slack through your belay device to give enough slack to create the MMO.

4. Transfer the weight back onto the climbing rope with the Munter tied with the cordelette and then remove the PMMO (fig. 3-17).

PRACTICE: BELAY ESCAPES

Practicing belay escapes is done much more effectively with a partner, but you can also use a heavy backpack if you can't find a willing guinea pig. Regardless of how confident you are, provide your guinea pig with a backup your first few times around. This can be done several ways:

1. If you have enough slack, you can tie the other end of the rope directly to the anchor and dangle it back down to your partner.
2. Have your partner tie in to the rope you will be practicing on and also *tether in* to the dangling line using a friction hitch. Leave enough slack so that you feel your partner's weight, but not so much that she would drop too far should you make a mistake.

If you do not have enough slack to drop down, you will need a second rope and preferably another anchor to help keep things clear and organized. Your partner can attach herself to the second line with a friction hitch, as described above.

Take the time to practice on a bottom anchor as if belaying a leader *and* up on the wall as if belaying a follower. Work your way up to practicing this on a hanging belay. Trying to escape a belay hanging in a harness is much more difficult than escaping a belay while standing on solid ground.

CHAPTER 4

Many successful ascents have been soured by descents gone awry. Pay just as much attention to how you'll get down as how you'll get up.

Descending

There are many different ways to descend, all of which are situation-dependent. In this chapter we discuss the important logistics, steps and considerations unique to lowering, rappelling, *tandem rappelling*, counterbalance rappelling, and pick-offs.

LOWERING

If the ground is close, lowering is usually the fastest way to get your partner (or partners) down in a hurry—no rappel ropes to deal with threading or throwing. Lowering can also create a viable exit for a follower unable to negotiate a tricky section of a route or for someone who has fallen into a crevasse and is able to walk out the bottom. Described below are a few different configurations to consider, dependent upon the climber's position as either leader or follower.

LOWERING MORE THAN ONE ROPE LENGTH

To lower from the top of a climb, set an anchor if you do not already have one, put the climber on belay on the anchor, and lower him down. This is a great technique if it is very windy and you are worried about your ropes getting stuck or your climber's ability to rappel.

Here is a step-by-step way to lower your partner two full rope lengths:

1. Tie two climbing ropes together (Rope A and Rope B).
2. Have your partner tie in to the end of Rope A. Tie the end of Rope B in to the anchor.
3. Tie a Munter to the anchor with Rope A.
4. On Rope B (just after the knot with Rope A) pre-rig a Munter-mule-overhand (MMO) clipped in to the anchor or shelf.

5. Lower your partner on Rope A until you run into the knot with Rope B. Have your partner unweight the rope by grabbing onto the rock, standing in the snow, etc. If your partner can't unweight the rope in this step, you will have to pass the knot (see chapter 7, Passing Knots).

6. Untie the Munter on Rope A, allowing the pre-rigged, tied-off MMO on Rope B to take the load.

7. Have your partner reweight the rope.

8. Remove the mule-overhand on Rope B and continue lowering your partner on Rope B's Munter.

9. To remove your partner from the system, she will have to either be on the ground or will have to make an anchor and clip in to it.

10. Your partner unties from Rope A so you can pull it up and do two double-rope rappels or a single rope rappel with a knot pass to reach her.

LOWERING WITH A SELF-BLOCKING BELAY DEVICE

Lowering a follower or providing slack on a self-blocking belay device like a Reverso or GiGi is not as easy as with a tubular belay device or a Munter hitch. (With a self-blocking

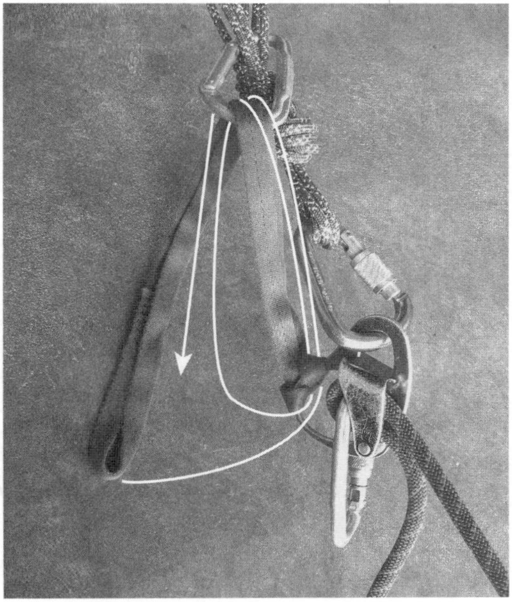

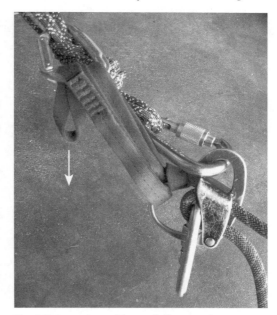

Fig. 4-1. Lowering with one follower using a self-blocking belay device: Step 1.

Fig. 4-2. Lowering with one follower using a self-blocking belay device: Step 2.

Fig. 4-3. Using body weight to release a self-blocking belay device.

belay device you will be belaying directly off the anchor.)

If your partner is not able to unweight the rope, follow the manufacturer's recommendations for lowering. Most devices require a cord to be attached to either the device or the blocking carabiner and then carefully levered to release the block. Each device is slightly different, so know your gear and follow the recommendations of the manufacturer.

LOWERING WITH ONE FOLLOWER

Let's first look at providing slack when belaying just one follower, using the Petzl Reverso in this example.

1. Girth-hitch a sling through the large metal loop on the Reverso. Clip a carabiner into the master point's (MP) shelf. Drape the sling through the carabiner (fig. 4-1).
2. Create a block and tackle by weaving the sling back and forth between the large loop on the Reverso and the carabiner (fig. 4-2). After a few wraps you should have enough leverage to pull down on the sling to release the belay device.

Important note: Remember to back the system up with a Munter tied with a carabiner on your belay loop; you are, after all, releasing your partner's belay. With the Munter you can feed out slack and lower your partner.

A variation on the above is, instead of doing a block and tackle, to use a long sling (or girth-hitch slings until you achieve the desired length) and step into the sling using your body weight to release the device (fig. 4-3). Again, remember to back the system up with a Munter and carabiner off your harness.

LOWERING WITH TWO FOLLOWERS

Say you are belaying two climbers on a self-blocking belay device; one needs slack while the other one wants to continue climbing. How will you provide slack to one without lowering the other? (The decision to belay two followers climbing at the same time is an advanced climbing technique with a variety of factors that need to be considered before implementing, which are outside the scope of this book. To learn more consult appendix D, Continuing Education).

1. Tie a mule overhand or a backup knot (clipped to the anchor) in the strand of rope going to the climber who does *not* wish to be lowered (fig. 4-4).
2. Lower the climber following your device manufacturer's recommendations. Make sure to provide slack to the correct side of the system—the climber who wanted slack in the first place. Remember to back the lower

Fig. 4-4. Lowering with two followers. The light rope (right) holds the climber who does not want to be lowered. This light rope is tied off with a mule overhand. A block and tackle is set up on the dark rope to lower the second climber.

up with a figure eight on a bight clipped to the MP or the Munter clipped to your belay loop depending on the length of the lower.

3. Once you have lowered your climber to the desired spot, tie a backup knot (clipped off to the anchor) or a mule overhand.
4. Carefully undo the backup knots while maintaining a hand on the brake strands. Make sure the belay device has re-engaged and then let her know that she can climb again.

LOWERING A LEADER

Lowering a leader is typically the fastest and simplest way to get your partner out of a tricky situation or help him with injuries.

LESS THAN HALF A ROPE LENGTH OUT

The easiest lowering situation involves a leader who is less than half a rope length up the next pitch, who needs help. If possible have your partner reinforce the piece of gear he is hanging on. Then just lower the lead climber back to the ledge or ground where you are. Careful! The lead climber can't be more than half a rope length up the route.

If the leader traveled over a roof or traversed to one side, it might be hard to get him back to the belay ledge. Try throwing excess rope or a long cordalette to him, then pull him in or have him help pull as you lower.

IMPROVISE: MUNTER POP

This useful rescue trick is a way to remove a loaded Munter from a carabiner. The pop can be used in a variety of situations. In this example it is being used to lower someone two rope lengths.

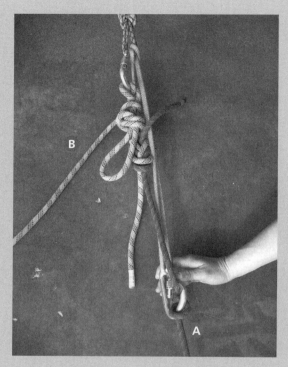

Tie the patient into the end of line A. Tie one end of line B to the anchor. Tie line B and line A together. On the MP put line B on belay (with a belay device or Munter hitch) just after the knot with line A and tie it off with a mule-overhand. Attach a two-foot sling to the MP and clip a locking carabiner to the end of the sling. Tie a Munter hitch in the end of line A attached to the patient and clip it to the locker on the sling. You are now ready to lower the patient off the Munter. Continue lowering the patient until all of line A is paid out. The tied-off belay device on line B is holding the load. The knot between the ropes is between the belay device and the carabiner

The Munter Pop set for the pop. The second rope is tied off and holding the load. Unclip the Munter strand and you are ready to lower on the second rope.

with the Munter. Now it is time for the Munter pop. Open the locking carabiner that has the Munter and pull the loaded line out of the gate. Let the gate close. If the carabiner does not flip around on its own, just bang it and it should pop and flip around. You can now unclip it from around rope A. Take out the mule-overhand backup and start lowering line B through the second Munter hitch.

To use the Munter pop you must have the first Munter loaded from both directions—in other words you must have a load hanging from the Munter and the brake strand (the side of the rope going up to the knot linking the two ropes) must be fully loaded and tied off as well.

If he is unable to help pull himself in, and he will not end up back on the ledge where you are, you will have to escape the belay. Ascend the line and attach a carabiner and sling to his side of the rope as soon as you can reach it (you do not necessarily have to ascend all the way up to him, but you do have to reach the side of rope that he has fallen onto). Descend back to the belay ledge and pull him in to the anchor as you lower. Be aware of any ledges the leader might hit as he is lowered. (See chapter 5, Ascending to a Hurt Leader, for details.)

MORE THAN HALF A ROPE LENGTH OUT

The hardest lowering situation is if the leader is more than half a rope length out. If possible have the leader reinforce the piece of gear he is hanging from, ideally creating an anchor into which he can clip himself and the climbing rope. Now escape the belay and ascend up the line. (See chapter 5, Ascending.)

If you have a second rope, you may be able to escape the belay and rope-solo or ascend the line a bit to remove enough of the low protection so that you will be able to lower him back to the belay ledge (or ground) using the two ropes tied together. Removing the low protection allows the knot linking the two ropes together to travel up toward the leader without getting stuck in the protection carabiners. Careful! Do not remove protection that might jeopardize the leader. He is hanging on one piece at the top of the system and a few pieces should be left to back that one up. You will have to pass the knot linking the two ropes as you lower the leader.

If you are uncomfortable removing your leader's pieces in order to allow the knot pass during a lower (perhaps he ran the pitch way out and there are just a few pieces to begin with), you will need to ascend or rope solo up to him.

RAPPELLING

Rappelling has multiple applications in a self-rescue scenario: it is used in tandem rappelling, counterbalance rappelling, and in the related topic of pick-offs. Let's first take a look at some common rappelling conundrums and solutions. Much of this first section lists some simple ways to avoid needing a rescue in the first place. Many climbers, especially alpine and traditional climbers, will testify that the majority of their rope mishaps have occurred while rappelling.

MANAGING RAPPEL ROPES

Stuck rappel lines are many climbers' public enemy number one. They have a sinister way of turning a nice outing into an epic! Here is a list of alternatives to simply throwing rappel lines—ideas worth considering, especially if you are rappelling a section where the rope could get easily snagged in deep cracks, on horns, bushes, or chicken heads, or be blown off course by strong winds. If you are rappelling a clean steep face or an overhang, you are less likely to run into problems.

RAPPELLING ON A MUNTER

In addition to being a way to belay, the Munter also provides an easy way to rig yourself either on a single- or double-strand rappel. When using two strands, just tie one big Munter with both strands at the same time (fig. 4-5). To minimize twists in the rope, keep your brake hand oriented directly in line under the carabiner and the Munters rather than off to the side.

Fig. 4-5. A two-strand Munter ready for rappelling. Caution! Note how the brake strand runs right next to the carabiner's gate. In positioning your brake hand take care that the brake strands do not run across the gate. Depending upon your carabiner's orientation the ropes could inadvertently unscrew the locker.

These tricks also have important rescue application: you do not want to further injure a patient by dislodging rocks, hitting him with airborne ropes, or risk a panicky climber grabbing the end of your rappel line, thereby inadvertently providing an unneeded *fireman's belay* (explained later in this chapter).

THE DIRECTED THROW

This method works well if it is not too windy and there are not too many things for the lines to get hung up on.

1. Set up the rappel as usual. Tie a knot near the rope's midpoint (or if a double-rope rappel, on one side of the knot linking the two ropes together) and clip that knot in to the anchor. This knot keeps the rope's midpoint in position while you throw the rope down. Otherwise the weight of thrown ropes can adjust the midpoint; you don't want to realize midrappel that your rope ends are uneven!

2. Make a set of very tight coils with each side of the rope—it works best to split each side into a set of anchor coils (the bit of rope from the anchor to about halfway to the end of the rope) and a set of end coils (end of the rope to about halfway to the anchor).

3. Overhand-throw the anchor coils directly where you want the line to go (or modify the direction to compensate for wind).

4. Throw the end coils based on what you learned with the first throw.

5. Repeat with the other side of the rappel ropes.

6. Untie the knot that keeps the midpoint in place and rappel.

THE HOLSTER METHOD

1. Carefully flake out each side of the rappel line separately, as if making a butterfly coil. Make sure that the end of the rope is on the bottom of the pile.

Fig. 4-6. The holster method. Each side of the rappel rope is neatly coiled and stored in holsters.

2. Girth-hitch a sling to a gear loop on either side of your harness.
3. Face the anchor and, while holding up the far side of the sling, lay the stack of rope into the sling at approximately the sling's midpoint.
4. Close the sling off by clipping the far side of the sling into a carabiner attached to the same gear loop you girth-hitched initially.
5. Repeat with the other side.
6. As you rappel, the rope will feed out of these holsters (fig. 4-6). Sometimes the rope gets tangled. Take a second to undo the snag and then keep rappelling. This method works well, though remember that some rope management must be done as you descend. With practice it is possible to set the holsters up with rope coils that will not tangle as easily. Be careful allowing a novice to do this. Use a rappel backup!

THE BACKPACK METHOD

1. Starting with both ends of the rappel line, create a stack inside the backpack. Do not pack the backpack so tightly that rope will not feed out freely as you rappel.
2. As you rappel stay ahead of the game by keeping a few feet of slack in the line between your belay device and your backpack (otherwise you will be caught fighting gravity with a taut line). Maintain your rappel with one hand and pull slack from the backpack with the other.

KEEPING ROPES FREE

Here are some other tips and tricks for good rope management and what to do when faced with stuck ropes.

Important Note: Do not rappel below any stuck section of your rope! Pause as you approach from above on rappel to free any stuck portions of rope.

- If the ropes run over an edge, think about extending the rappel even if this means leaving a sling behind; it could be well worth it, particularly if you've tied two ropes together and are concerned about the knot getting caught as it pulls over the lip. The friction generated by pulling the rope over the edge may make it difficult to retrieve.

- Choose a low-profile knot if tying two ropes together (e.g. Flemish bend or overhand, aka eurodeath knot).

- Before the last person rappels have someone below check the pull of the ropes. If it looks like there are going to be any problems, then the person up top can make adjustments before going down.

- Make sure you are pulling the correct strand down if you have knotted two ropes together and check that there are no twists in the ropes.

- Depending on the length of the rappel, it is possible to move the rappel knot past an offending edge by adjusting the ropes. It is even possible for the last rappeller to stop a little way down and readjust the ropes, moving the knot over any problem spots. Careful! Doing this makes the rope ends uneven. Only do this if you have knots in the end of your rope or

know you have plenty of slack to reach the next rappel station.

- If the rappel station is set up so that one of the rope strands will run against the rock and the other will be stacked on top of it, set the ropes up so that you will pull the strand that hangs against the rock. If you pull the outer strand it can sometimes pinch the inner one at the anchor and make it difficult to pull.

- When rappelling with two ropes in windy situations, position the knot on the upwind side of the rappel anchor. When you pull the ropes, the free line blows downwind and is easy to pull through the anchor. If it is set up the other way, when the free line blows downwind, it can put almost a full wrap onto the anchor and adds quite a bit of friction, especially if there are any twists in the lines.

- If possible, change your position if you encounter resistance: move farther away from the wall and/or try moving to either the right or the left.

Getting Ropes Unstuck and Last Resorts

When ropes do get stuck, try the following:

- If you still have both ends of the rappel line, sometimes it helps to pull the rope back up a bit—pulling on the other strand can actually help free the stuck side.

- Flick the rope from left to right, up and down. Give yourself enough slack to create a wavelike motion with the rope.

- As a last resort, tug in all directions with all of your and your partner's might.

Watch for whipping rope ends and even more dangerous, dislodged rocks!

If you can't get your ropes unstuck, here are a few options:

- If both strands are still with you, tie a friction hitch (like a Prusik) around both strands of rope and free-climb or ascend (see chapter 5) back up the rappel route, pushing the Prusiks up the line with you as you climb. If you are reclimbing a route that is only typically used for descents, take care; the rocks may be much looser than you would find on an ascent line.

- If only one strand is available, then you may have enough rope to reload the pitch. If you can't free-climb the pitch, remember that French-freeing or aiding back up is always an option! (See chapter 5 for a description of *French-freeing*.) Attach a Prusik to the stuck rope and slide it up as you go as a backup.

- If only one strand of the rappel line is available and you do not have enough slack to lead the pitch, or if the terrain is too difficult to free or aid climb (while pushing a Prusik up the line as described in the first example), then you are looking at ascending the rope using an *ascension rig* (see chapter 5, Ascending). This is a scary proposition, since you have no idea what your rope is stuck on and therefore no idea what will be holding your weight. Build an anchor and have your partner clip in to the anchor and tie in to the bottom of the stuck line on which you will be *prusiking*. Have him put the stuck line (you) on belay. You will ascend the line with your ascension rig (rather than being tied in to the rope, you are attached via your ascension rig). Place gear at any available opportunity and clip the rope you are ascending to it; this way if the rope does dislodge, you will take a leader fall, or at worst a fall on the anchor, which is not great but is better than plummeting down multiple pitches with the freed climbing rope.

- A minor saving grace with this option is that if you and your partner tugged as hard as you could and the rope still would not budge, hopefully that means the rope is good and stuck. That being said this is *not* an option to be taken lightly. Do not rule out the idea of cutting the rope and continuing to descend with whatever portion of rope you have left.

- If it so happens that you are stuck with only one strand but are not too far off the ground, consider rappelling on the available side of rope. Build an anchor and fix the available strand of rope to the anchor's MP. Rappel down on the single strand. This solution does mean leaving gear and your rope; certainly costly, but still potentially lower than the price of higher-risk options.

RAPPEL BACKUP

Many climbers view rappelling as one of the most vulnerable moments of a climb. A climber is no longer relying on good movement as her primary means of safety; in-

Fig. 4-7. Fireman's belay. The climber on the ground provides a belay by pulling downward on the two rappel strands.

stead she is completely relying on an artificial system. Imagine if a rock fell from above and crashed into your arm (or knocked you unconscious), or a wasp took you by surprise with a sharp bite. Would you maintain your brake hand? Hard to say. Imagine if your hand came off even for a second. What would happen? Or what if you had not tied knots in the ends of your rappel line and you did not notice you were at the end until you only had a few inches left to go? Many people have died this way. If you are on belay during the climb you are backed up for

these eventualities. It makes sense to back yourself up for the rappel as well.

Personal comfort level and perceived risk dictates whether or not you choose to employ a backup, but in a rescue setting it is a certainly a good idea. With adrenaline pumping and seldom-used systems put into operation under tense circumstances, it can be easy to make a mistake. You are also taking responsibility for someone else's well-being, not just your own. Finally, think of all the tasks you may need to accomplish with your hands; having a backup already in place will speed up the process of freeing your hands.

FIREMAN'S BELAY

This is an extremely fast and simple backup. Just have someone located on the ground (or at the anchor you are rappelling down to) hold both rope strands, leaving a little bit of slack in the line (fig. 4-7). Should you need to stop and free your hands (or suddenly get hit in the head by a large chunk of falling ice), your belayer simply yanks downward, their pull acting as a remote brake hand. When you want to continue rappelling, your belayer simply lets up a bit on the rope. (You maintain your own brake hand, feeding slack through your rappel device as you descend.) As a backup belayer take care that you are out of harm's way as best you can from rock fall or other debris.

THIRD HAND

A *third hand* is a friction hitch tied with a rescue loop or runner around both brake strands below the rappel device. With a regular rappel setup, it can be attached to a harness' leg loop. Or, the belay device can be set on a *cow's tail* (described later in this chapter) and the third hand attached to the harness' belay loop.

1. With a rescue loop or a runner, wrap an autoblock around both brake strands and clip the rescue loop in to your harness' leg loop with a locking carabiner (fig. 4-8).
2. Keep your brake hand just above the autoblock (closest to the rappel device). If you rappel at an even pace, taking care to feed the rope through

the third hand with a smooth motion, your autoblock will be less likely to catch unwantedly, resulting in a smoother, more comfortable rappel.

If you need to stop and get your hands free, all you have to do is gradually let go and make sure the autoblock engages.

Another viable option for a third hand is tying a Prusik around the two brake strands (again, below your belay device) with a piece of cord (the cord does not need to be tied into a loop). Thread one side of the cord through your harness' leg loop and simply connect it to the other strand of cord

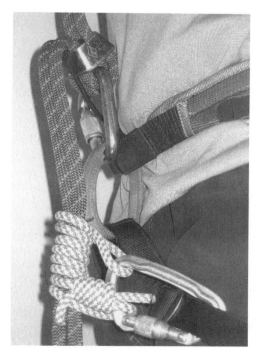

Fig. 4-8. Third hand. An autoblock clipped to the leg loop with a locking carabiner.

Fig. 4-9. Third-hand variation. Using a short cord, tie a Prusik around the brake strands, then tie the cord off to the harness' leg loop with an overhand.

with an overhand or figure eight on a bight. This eliminates the need for a carabiner. (See fig. 4-9.)

As whenever using friction hitches, test your hitch with a quick tug in the direction of pull and make sure it catches. This is especially necessary if using ropes that are new and slippery or of two different diameters.

RAPPELLING WITH A COW'S TAIL

A cow's tail is a tether or single sling girth-hitched on a harness' belay loop with a locking carabiner and attached to the other end of the sling. In this case the locking carabiner that would typically clip through your belay loop (then into the rappel device and rope) connects the cow's tail to a rappel device.

1. Girth-hitch a runner around your belay loop, creating a cow's tail.
2. Load your rappel device with the rope as you normally do for belaying.
3. Clip a locking carabiner through the rappel device and rope, then through the cow's tail instead of the belay loop.

It is easy to employ the use of a third hand in this setup. You can clip the third hand right to your belay loop. See fig. 4-10 showing a rappel using a cow's tail. Note the climber pushing down her third hand (right hand) as she rappels.

A cow's tail serves multiple purposes: The rappel device is further removed from the waist/chest area and therefore objects like clothing, long hair, and skin are less likely to get caught. It is less cumbersome to deal with when paying out rope as you rappel (especially if you are rappelling with your ropes stacked in holsters) or when

Fig. 4-10. Cow's tail. "A" indicates the rappel device and locking carabiner; "B" indicates the cow's tail; "C" indicates the rappeller's third-hand rappel backup.

managing a third hand, and the uncluttered space created by using a cow's tail can make rappelling with a patient much more manageable.

Using a cow's tail also provides an easy way to leave a rappeller unsupervised and ready to rappel, without relying on him to safely rig himself in to the system. Once the climber is rigged on rappel with a cow's tail, you can rappel first. The downward pull on the ropes created by the weight of the first rappeller functions as a lock-off on the second rappeller's brake strands—just like a fireman's belay. (The cow's tail creates an extension that prevents the second climber from getting sucked into the rock.) Once the first rappeller is done rappelling and her weight is taken off the rope, the second rappeller has enough slack necessary for rappelling. *Important Note:* Careful about unweighting the rope midrappel. As soon as the first rappeller unweights the rappel rope the second person's rappel can be initiated.

TANDEM RAPPELLING

Tandem rappelling involves rappelling with two people using the same device. This is a great technique for descending with an injured, unskilled, or incapacitated person, or when completing a "pick-off" (described later in this chapter). The easiest way to rig a tandem rappel uses two separate tethers. This is where a Purcell Prusik (see the Purcell Prusik sidebar) comes in handy providing an adjustable tether for the rescuer. Adjustable tethers allow you to change your position in relation to your patient and the terrain, thereby allowing a more comfortable descent for you and your patient. Although using a tether is simple and fast, it does not provide you with an easy way to transfer your and your patient's weight on and off the anchor (see fig. 4-11).

1. Girth-hitch a runner through your partner's belay loop, creating a cow's tail.
2. Girth-hitch your Purcell Prusik (or cow's tail) through your belay loop and extend it so you will hang slightly below your patient once on rappel.
3. Load the rappel device with the rope.
4. Clip both you and your patient's cara-

Fig. 4-11. Starting a tandem rappel. This photo provides a good view of tandem rappelling and the use of two separate cow's tails, one for each rappeller. The attendant (left) stands behind the patient (right) with legs staggered to provide support as they move over the edge.

biners through the rope and the rappel device. The two carabiners add friction to the system and make it easier to control the double load. They also allow you and your patient to be on independent systems. If two isn't enough, you can always consider a third carabiner.
5. Once you both unclip from the anchor you are ready to rappel.

STARTING THE RAPPEL
Leaning back over the edge can be one of the most difficult parts of tandem rappelling.
1. Get behind your patient.
2. With each of you standing in a

THE PURCELL PRUSIK

The Purcell Prusik, developed by British Columbia's Columbia Mountain Rescue Group, is an excellent multiuse tool for improvised rescue and personal climbing application. The Purcell functions both as an adjustable tether that can be used for clipping in to an anchor (or a rappel device) and also for ascending a fixed line. It does take more cord to tie than other ascension rigs (see chapter 5, Ascending), but its multipurpose nature makes it very versatile. It can always be untied and used as a cordalette as well.

The Purcell setup consists of three different lengths of cord tied to create two separate foot Prusiks of different lengths and one waist Prusik. Here we explain how to tie a foot Purcell Prusik (in improvised rescue, just one foot Purcell can be adequate); this length can be used as a tether (aka cow's tail) or as a foot Prusik for ascension. Measurements for the waist Prusik (same as the one employed in other improvised ascension rigs) are discussed in chapter 5, Ascending.

Depending on your height you will need 12–15 feet of cord.

1. Tie a figure eight on a bight, incorporating both ends of the cordelette (similar to a Frost knot). The resulting smaller bight should be approximately 8 inches in diameter (figs. 4-12 and 4-13). This loop ("A" in the figures) will be attached to the rope with a Prusik for ascending or can be girth-hitched through a harness' belay loop for use as a tether.
2. With the bigger loop ("B" in the figures) create the skeleton of a three-wrap Prusik on your index finger and thumb (fig. 4-14). Wrap the cord around your fingers starting the wrap on the outside of your fingers and finishing on the inside. Move up the length of your fingers toward your fingertips.
3. Bring your fingertips together. Then slide two fingers in through the loops to facilitate step 4.
4. Thread loop "A" through the Prusik skeleton you have just created (fig. 4-15). Pull through the Prusik all but a few inches at the end.
5. Grab the two strands exiting the Prusik ("C" in fig. 4-16) and pull them directly downward. Tailor the length of your Purcell to your body by feeding slack through the Prusik; adjust tail length of the figure eight if necessary. Fig. 4-17 shows a completed, long Purcell Prusik.

The loop created with the Prusik hitch can be cinched down around your foot for ascension purposes or can be clipped with a carabiner when used as a tether. When used as a tether, a simple slide of the Prusik adjusts the tether's length.

Fig. 4-12. Step 1.

Fig. 4-13: Step 1, completed. "A" indicates the smaller loop; "B" indicates the larger loop.

Fig. 4-14. Step 2 (Step 3 not shown).

Fig. 4-15. Step 4.

Fig. 4-16. Step 5 "C" indicates the two strands exiting the Prusik.

Fig. 4-17. A completed long Purcell Prusik.

shoulder-width stance, alternate your legs. Each of you should have one leg on the outside of the stance.

3. Lean back and lower or rappel as normal.

RESCUE SPIDER

The *rescue spider* is another simple way to quickly rig for a tandem rappel. It has a number of advantages: it connects the rescuer and the patient while requiring only one sling; it allows attachment for a rappel device; it has a long tail for transferring both climbers onto an anchor with a releasable hitch. These attributes make transitions to and from multiple rappel anchors quick and simple. Its only drawback is that its tether lengths are fixed. It is not as easy as a Purcell to adjust your position relative to your patient once connected.

Building a Rescue Spider

1. Use a long rescue cordelette (about 20 feet) tied in a loop with a Flemish bend.
2. Double the loop over and tie a figure eight on a bight so that you are left with three loops, one long and two short (one of which will have two loops of its own—a result of tying the bight). One short loop should be about 1 foot long, the other short loop should be about 1.5 feet long, and the long loop should be about 3–5 feet long. (The figure eight bend should not be on the long loop; it should be in one of the two shorter loops).
3. Clip locking carabiners in to the two shorter loops (fig 4.18). These carabi-

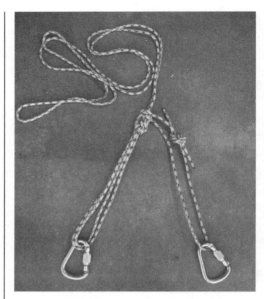

Fig.4-18. A tied rescue spider. Patient and rescuer each have a carabiner to clip into.

ners clip in to your harness and your patient's. Clip the 1.5-foot loop in to your harness. (It is possible to tie knots in this loop to shorten it up in case you want to be in front of your patient during parts of the descent. That technique is not shown.)

Using the Rescue Spider

In this scenario we assume you are setting up for a tandem rappel with your patient.

1. Set up your rescue spider (fig. 4-18) and clip the 1.5-foot loop to your harness. Clip the shorter loop in to your patient's harness.
2. Build an anchor and place a locking carabiner on the MP (fig. 4-19).

USING THE RESCUE SPIDER

Fig. 4-19. Steps 2 and 3: (not yet tied off with a mule-overhand).

Fig. 4-20. Step 3 complete. You and your patient can now weight the anchor (step 4 not shown).

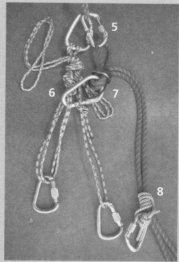

Fig. 4-21. Steps 5, 6, 7, and 8.

Fig. 4-22. Step 9

Fig. 4-23. Step 10

3. Attach the spider to the anchor using the spider's long loop to tie a MMO (fig. 4-20).
4. You can now weight the anchor and hang from the spider.
5. Set your rope up for rappel on the anchor (fig. 4-21).
6. Attach a locking carabiner to the rescue spider through the two tether loops connecting you and your partner, below the large figure eight knot (fig. 4-21).
7. Set up the rappel device on the rope (fig. 4-21). Use two locking carabiners here instead of one for extra friction, especially if dealing with a heavy patient.
8. Attach a third hand to the rappel ropes and clip it to your harness belay loop (fig. 4-21).
9. Release the mule-overhand and lower your weight onto the rappel device (fig. 4-22). Make sure the third hand engages, holding the load.
10. Remove the Munter and take the extra locker from the anchor (fig. 4-23). Rappel to the next station.

Repeat these steps at each station until you reach the ground.

RAPPEL POSITIONING IN RELATION TO A PATIENT

There are a variety of ways to position yourself in relation to your patient—all depending upon you and your patient's height and weight, the terrain you are rappelling through, and the severity of your patient's injuries. Here are some considerations.

In the Lap

If your patient is the same size or smaller than you, suffers from injuries that you need to keep your hands on, or you need to provide head support while rappelling, place him perpendicular to your body in your lap. If your partner is significantly larger or heavier than you it can be difficult to negotiate lower-angle terrain in this position. If you have short legs it can be tough to rappel over roofs or to rely on your legs for control in this position.

Side by Side

If your partner is physically able, this is a good option for rappelling down lower-angle terrain. You are able to coach and physically support your partner if need be. Depending upon the severity of the situation, some patients may appreciate the relative sense of control that using their feet provides. It also may be less taxing for you as a rescuer—something important to keep in mind especially if you have a long descent. From the side-by-side position it is easy to move into a staggered rappel position (see fig. 4-11, earlier this chapter) to help your patient negotiate terrain features and complete edge transitions.

Piggyback

Once in motion on the rope, gently swing your patient around onto your back. (This sounds more difficult than it actually is.) This technique works especially well when the rescuer is smaller than the patient. The cow's tail holds the patient's weight while you simply keep the patient in place with

EDGE TRANSITIONS

Edge transitions can be tricky, particularly if more than one person is on the line. These transitions are awkward and pose definite risks to the rescuer and/or patient: a slip, or even too quick a transition while moving over the edge, puts more force on the anchor as the climber's weight drops and there is the potential for injury or rope damage. Here are some tricks for making your edge transitions smoother:

Try to rig high: This can lessen the sharpness of the angle created by the rope going over an edge. Setting the anchor higher also reduces the amount of friction added to the system by the rope running over the edge (making hauling easier) and can protect the rope from abrasion or an abrupt transition.

Consider edge protection: It is worth emphasizing that your ropes are your lifelines. Do what you can to protect them! If the rope moves over a sharp lip, pad the area with backpacks, extra clothing, a rope bag—whatever you have available (don't forget to attach these items to the anchor). Due to the way the rope's core is constructed, lateral movement over sharp protrusions running perpendicular to a rope are much more damaging than a protrusion running parallel. This is particularly important as you add more weight into the system (i.e., two people hanging off the system instead of just one).

a piggyback. Because there is nothing between you and the wall, you can easily negotiate terrain. Once you and your patient reach the next belay station (or the ground), swing your patient back around in front, positioning him either hip-to-hip with you or with your legs staggered as explained in "Starting the Rappel," earlier this chapter.

COUNTERBALANCE RAPPELLING

The counterbalance rappel is a good method to use when you know you need to descend to a patient and will continue down to him. This is a technically involved skill, and care should be used when executing it. It is fast and efficient when employed correctly, and it is mostly used in emergency (injury) situations so it should be practiced thoroughly.

Counterbalance rappels are rigged so that the rope can be pulled and retrieved once the rappel is complete. (If you anticipate needing to raise your patient, a single strand rappel, tied off to the anchor, may make more sense.) This method works even if there is only one rope and the second is more that half a rope length down.

1. If belaying off the anchor (as shown in figs. 4-25–4-32), get hands-free ("1A" in fig. 4-25) and back up the belay ("1B" in fig. 4-26). If belaying off your harness, get hands-free and then follow slightly different steps, described second in the steps that

follow, until step 6. In either case, reinforce the anchor if necessary. Two people's weight will be hanging on the anchor with the forces of a lower and a rappel.

2. Attach a cordelette using a PMMO between the load strand and the anchor for load transfer ("2A" and "2B" in fig. 4-26).

3. Lower your climber onto the PMMO setup (fig. 4-27). (If using a self-blocking belay device like a Reverso you may need to employ the steps for lowering described earlier in this chapter if you are unable to manually release the belay device.)

4. Clip a locking carabiner through the anchor's MP (fig. 4-28) and clip in the section of rope running between the loaded Prusik and the belay backup knot. If you were belaying off your harness, you can clip the rope between the loaded Prusik and the tied-off belay into the locking carabiner. This is your new MP.

5. Thread the rope through your rappel device ("5A" in fig. 4-28). Attach a third hand to your brake strand ("5B" in fig. 4-29). Gather all gear and equipment, as you will not return to this spot. If you were belaying off your harness, you are already set to rappel.

6. Remove the belay backup knot and take up the slack through your Munter (fig. 4-29). If you were belaying off your harness, you should be slack-free already.

7. Weight your side of the rappel setup and undo your anchor tie-off or tether

so you are ready to rappel down the rope (fig. 4-29).

8. Undo the MMO tied onto the load strand with the cordelette and slowly lower your patient's weight onto the climbing rope (fig. 4-30). You are the counterbalance, so make sure you weight the other side or you will be pulled up to the anchor carabiners.

9. Leave the Prusik (of the PMMO setup) on the patient's rope ("9A" in fig. 4-31). Clip the other end of the cordelette in to a locker on your belay loop ("9B" in fig. 4-31). This connection allows you to stay in control of both ropes. It is very important you remember to slide the Prusik connected to your partner's side of the rope down the line with you as you rappel.

10. Rappel as far as you can until you reach your patient or you run into your tie-in at the other end of the rope.

If you have not reached your patient you must build another anchor and repeat the above steps. Steps for building another anchor follow. Skip to step 22 if you reach your patient.

11. Make sure your third hand grabs and get hands-free.

12. Build an anchor.

13. Clip yourself in to the anchor with your tether, but do not weight it.

14. Use a spare cordelette to attach your patient's side of the rope to the anchor by tying a PMMO combination onto a locking carabiner clipped through the MP.

15. Slowly feed out rope through your rappel device so your patient's weight

is transferred to the cordelette (and thereby the anchor) along with your weight transferring onto your tether.

16. On your patient's side of the rope, above the loaded Prusik, tie a figure eight on a bight and clip it to the MP; this serves as a backup to the cordelette.

17. Untie the rope from your harness.

18. Pull the rope through the first anchor and rethread it through the anchor you are hanging on.

19. Tie in to the end of the rope (or tie a stopper knot at the end of the rope) and set yourself up to rappel. Set your third hand so you can be hands-free.

20. Make sure all slack is out of the rappel system and you have everything you need. Release the PMMO tied on your patient's side of the rope, lowering your patient's weight onto the other side of the MP.

21. Unclip your tether and clip it to your patient's side of the line as you rappel, taking care to slide it down with you as you descend.

You now have much more rope and will hopefully reach your patient without having to do this all again—though you might! In which case, repeat steps 11 through 21.

22. Once you have reached your patient you must build another anchor and transfer both of you to it (fig. 4-32). Then pull the rope down through the last anchor and continue by means of tandem rappelling. For efficiency, use a rescue spider to connect you and your patient together as well as to transfer your weight on and off the anchor for rappelling.

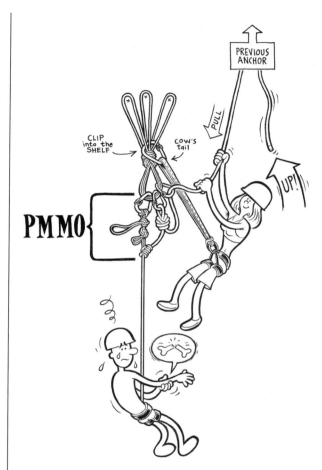

Fig. 4-24. Counterbalance rappelling. Steps 1-18 completed. The rescuer was not able to reach her patient with just one counterbalance rappel so she is taking the steps necessary to set up a second counterbalance rappel. She has built a new anchor to which she and her patient are attached (her patient with a releasable hitch.) She is now pulling the rope through the anchor above in order to rappel off the new anchor.

COUNTERBALANCE RAPPELLING

Fig. 4-25. Step 1A. Get hands-free.

Fig. 4-26. Steps 1B, 2A, 2B. Back up the belay; attach a PMMO (Prusik, 2A; Munter-mule-overhand, 2B).

Fig. 4-27. Step 3. Transfer the load to the PMMO, in this case by levering the self-blocking belay device using the striped sling.

Fig. 4-28. Steps 4 and 5A. Set up to rappel. Thread the rope through your rappel device.

Fig. 4-29. Steps 5B, 6 and 7. Attach a third hand to your brake strand. Take out all slack and leave a good anchor.

Fig. 4-30. Step 8.

Fig. 4-31. Steps 9A and 9B. The Prusik is on the patient's rope (9A) and the other end of the cordelette is clipped in to a locker on your belay loop (9B).

Fig. 4-32. Step 10: Counterbalance to tandem rappelling. Attach to the patient and get onto an anchor. Note: If you were unable to reach your patient in one counterbalance rappel you will have to continue counterbalance rappelling (see Fig. 4-24). Step 10 assumes you are at your partner.

ANCHOR-BUILDING TECHNIQUES

Stand on your bathroom scale and quickly drop down to your knees. Notice how you can cause the dial to spike way beyond your actual weight? The same effect happens when you bounce on a climbing rope or an anchor. (The effect is dampened by a variety of factors, for example the amount of rope active in the system.) Now imagine that effect with two climbers relying on the system. The amount of weight your anchor experiences increases dramatically. Therefore, before continuing with a rescue it may be necessary to reinforce your anchor or at the least evaluate your anchor's vector angles, sling craft, and position, particularly if you will be raising or counterbalance rappelling.

SLING CRAFT

A well-thought-out rescue anchor can become a bit more complicated than simply slinging a bunch of pieces together. The amount of cordage used in linking pieces in anchor construction affects how much force is transferred to each individual piece. (See fig. 4-33.)

As Mike Gibbs of Rigging for Rescue puts it, think about stretching out one side of a rubber band. Now stretch both sides of the rubber band using the same amount of force. It does not stretch as far. This same principle applies to the cordelette used in anchor construction.

The more material an anchor point has (as compared to other anchor points in the system), the less that anchor point's material will stretch when the anchor is loaded. The less an anchor point can stretch, the higher the force that will be transferred to that anchor point's piece of protection. (The principle is similar to the difference between taking a big lead fall on a static rope versus a dynamic one. A static rope delivers a much higher jolt to your body while the dynamic rope stretches, dampening the effects of the fall.) Therefore, an easy way to maximize the use of stronger pieces in your anchor system (like a big bottleneck hex in perfect rock) is to bring more material (webbing or cord) to that particular anchor point.

Take a look at the center anchor in Figure 4-33. The middle anchor point has two strands of webbing compared with just the one strand comprising both outside anchor points. This means that more force will be transferred to the anchor's middle point, and less to the outside points (they have less material) due to the differences in elongation (excluding differences in vector angles).

A separate consideration, not to be confused with the elongation principles information explained above, is that the material linking the middle anchor point to the master point has a stronger strength rating than that of the outside anchor points. A single strand of 7-mm knotless cordelette is rated for 10 kiloNewtons (kN) while a doubled-over section of cord (as shown in the center anchor point) can handle double the load (less the strength reduction for the knot).

CARABINER LOADING

Considering that you are more likely to repeatedly weight and unweight the anchor in a rescue scenario (think of all the repositioning down below that might go on with a patient), it is important to keep the possibility of cross-loading or triaxial loading carabiners in mind. *Cross-loading* refers to loading a carabiner across its short axis (over its gate.) *Triaxial loading* refers to loading a carabiner in three directions at the same time rather than the two directions it is designed for. When the tension on a system is relaxed and then reapplied, a carabiner can slip into a dangerous orientation. This is one of the reasons why being tight on your anchor is always emphasized. Take care to rig conservatively and with this consideration in mind.

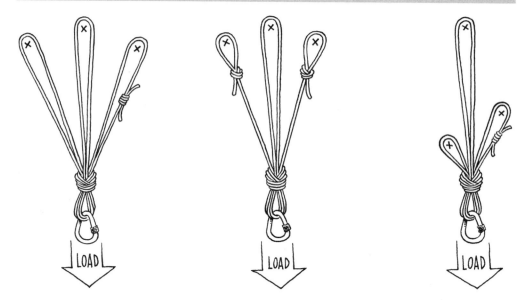

Fig. 4-33. **Left Anchor:** *All three anchor points are equal in amount of available material. Force will be distributed equally throughout this anchor. Compare this to the right anchor where all three anchor points are different lengths.*

Center Anchor: *Although the anchor component lengths are similar, the outside components have one strand of cordelette while the inside has two. Because the inside anchor point has more available material it will stretch less.*

Right anchor: *The anchor components are unequal so they will see unequal loading. The shortest will see the most load and the longest will see the least load.*

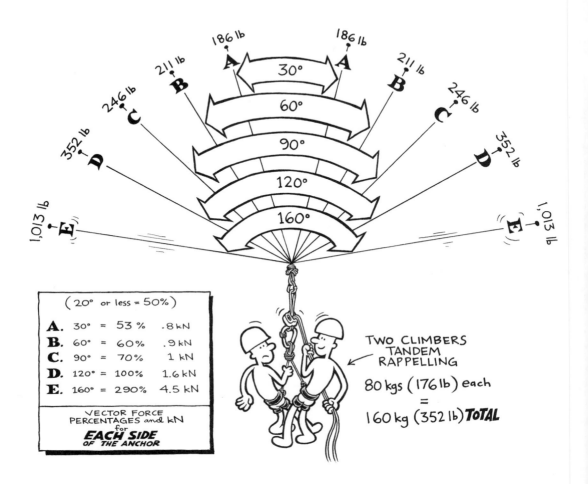

186 lb   186 lb

211 lb   211 lb

246 lb   246 lb

352 lb   352 lb

1,013 lb   1,013 lb

A   A   30°

B   B   60°

C   C   90°

D   D   120°

E   E   160°

(20° or less = 50%)

A. 30° = 53% .8 kN
B. 60° = 60% .9 kN
C. 90° = 70% 1 kN
D. 120° = 100% 1.6 kN
E. 160° = 290% 4.5 kN

VECTOR FORCE
PERCENTAGES and kN
for
EACH SIDE
OF THE ANCHOR

TWO CLIMBERS
TANDEM
RAPPELLING

80 kgs (176 lb) each
=
160 kg (352 lb) TOTAL

Fig. 4-34. Here's a good look at why building a solid anchor is so important. For testing purposes the UIAA uses 80 kilograms (176 lb) as a climber's weight. We have increased that to 160 kilograms (352 lb), because many rescues involve the weight of two climbers on the system. Look at the different amounts of force each anchor component will receive as the vector angle increases. Although quality gear in quality rock can certainly withstand these forces, this demonstrates why building with small vector angles (particularly in snow, poor rock, or ice) is important.

PICK-OFFS

A *pick-off* is the process of a rescuer either rappelling or being lowered down to a stranded or injured person (could be a climber or even a hiker that got in over his head) and "picking him off" the wall.

Our discussion of pick-offs assumes the rescuer is using a single rope. Search and rescue (SAR) teams typically use two-rope techniques: a main line and a belay. Those systems are beyond the scope of this book. There are many good classes referenced in appendix D, Continuing Education.

You might use a pick-off to deal with a situation involving your party—rock fall severing a rope, for example. More likely you will use it to help another party. It is a great skill to know and one of the basics of organized search and rescue.

PICK-OFF PREP

It is important to think and plan a little before jumping over the edge to help someone. Before you descend, consider the following:

- Should you bring any supplies down with you? For example: first-aid supplies, specific medication, extra layers, food and water, a harness or material to make a harness with, material for a chest harness, extra gear for creating an anchor or reinforcing the injured climber's gear.
- If someone has accompanied you to the site, how will you communicate with him or her?
- Although obviously subject to change, what is your plan of action?

- Before you set an anchor consider where it lies in relation to the patient. If possible set it off slightly to either side; you do not want ropes or loose debris to hit your patient. Off-setting the rope to one side also lessens the risk of a panicky patient grabbing your lines. (Another way to avoid both of these hazards is to keep the rope strands with you as you rappel, in either a holster or a backpack as discussed in the Rappelling section.) However, do not set your anchor so far off to the side that reaching your patient turns into a struggle.
- It might be necessary to spend a little time clearing out potential hazards (loose rocks, deadfall, etc.) that could fall on you and your patient.
- Is the anchor strong and secure enough to withstand the forces of raising should you and the patient need to be hauled?
- If rappelling, rig your rappel device on an adjustable tether and pre-rig a fixed-length tether for your patient. Or use a rescue spider. (Run the rappel rope through two carabiners. The additional friction will help control the weight of two climbers.)

THE PICK-OFF

When executing a pick-off, you want to be able to clip the patient in to a rope as quickly as possible. Be aware that as you approach your patient he may, out of panic or relief, grab at you, creating an obstacle that makes it difficult for you to rappel or to clip in to him. In this type of situation you should be very direct: tell the patient exactly what you want him to do. Again, your first objective will typically be to get the patient clipped in to your system as soon as possible.

Once you have reached your patient, clip the free locking carabiner coming off the tether (or rescue spider) in to your patient's belay loop, or secure him into an improvisational harness (as described below in "Safely Assisting and Rigging an Injured Climber").

In all likelihood it will make most sense to untie your patient from his climbing rope, as he is now clipped in to your system. But do not simply untie him as a matter of course—consider if this is in fact what makes the most sense. And of course, double-check that he is correctly clipped in to your system before untying anything. Your patient will need to unweight his rope in order to facilitate untying from it.

From this point you have a variety of options: perhaps you build an anchor and pull the rope (or it is dropped down to you if you are being lowered) and continue via tandem rappel (see "Rappel Positioning in Relation to a Patient" and "Tandem Rappelling" earlier this chapter); maybe you prepare for a raise; or it may be that the best solution is to continue down the rest of the rope's length via either lowering or rappelling.

This pick-off process will be essentially the same whether you are being lowered down by a third party from above or rappelling.

SAFELY ASSISTING AND RIGGING AN INJURED CLIMBER

If you are descending to a patient who is not wearing a harness (e.g., an adventurous kid stranded on a ledge), bring something you can loop around her quickly, such as a sewn or tied double-length runner. Loop it around her waist and clip the rope in to her immediately. If she were to take a small stumble or fall, the loop would slide up her body, stopped by her armpits. This is of course only a temporary solution. Then you can take the time to tie an improvised harness (like the diaper harness described below) or to fit the patient in a manufactured one.

The injured party may also require additional support. Described below are a variety of sling, chest, and seat harnesses—all built with a limited amount of tools, most involving nothing more than a cordelette or webbing. Although there are few situations when you actually need to use these tools, they are useful to know. If moving in tandem with your patient, you obviously will be able to provide her with plenty of support using your own body. But what happens when you reach an anchor and your hands need to switch from stabilizing your patient to rigging tasks? This is exactly the type of instance where these particular techniques come in handy. You can pay full attention to your anchor transition, knowing that your patient is still in a stable and supported position.

As with any improvised rescue, there is no perfect answer. For assisting and rigging an injured climber, the solution depends on what gear and outside resources (bystanders or rescue teams) you have available, the climber's injuries, and the terrain over which you will be moving your patient.

These descriptions exclude first-aid information, in particular the important step

HARNESS HANG SYNDROME

Although rare, harness hang syndrome is worth being aware of. It occurs when someone is left hanging from a rope immobile in a harness and can result in death. More commonly recognized among cavers, the syndrome has indeed occurred in climbing situations. The syndrome is believed to be caused by the harness trapping blood in the legs and as a result not enough blood gets to the brain; a change in blood chemistry is also indicated, and it is believed that the situation overall can be exacerbated by exhaustion or cold. But no one is certain what causes the syndrome and theories vary. Tests conducted at the Aerospace Medical Research Lab at the Wright-Patterson Air Force Base found that symptoms onset in an average of six minutes. Symptoms begin as a general feeling of flulike illness and progress to excessive sweating, nausea, dizziness, and hot flashes followed by unconsciousness. Even the slightest movement can help avoid this. If a patient is caught hanging in a harness the bottom line is to get to your patient as quickly as possible.

of evaluating and treating for spinal injury. Refer to the Continuing Education and Recommended Reading appendixes for more information on wilderness first aid.

Diaper Harness

A diaper seat is an acceptable quick harness. This harness is quick and more secure than just a sling around a patient's waist, but it is not a foolproof harness. Tying a Swiss seat or having a second harness for the patient will be preferable if you need to perform a long lower or raise; if you are assisting someone without a harness, try to borrow someone else's to take with you to the patient.

For the diaper harness, you will need a double- or triple-length sling tied or sewn in a loop (about 4 feet long when tied).

1. Put the loop around the patient's waist like you are putting on a belt (do not put it over her head).
2. Grab one of the loop's strands and pull it up through the patient's legs.
3. Bring the bight you just pulled between the patient's legs and the two bights created by the end of the loop, resting on either side of her waist, together at her belly button.
4. Adjust the strand going around the patient's back so it is snug; the excess slack should come out in the bight between her legs.
5. Depending on the patient's size you can just clip the three bights together with a locking carabiner, or you can tie knots to shorten the webbing for a snug fit and then clip. If the patient is too big for the diaper, just wrap her waist and use another piece of webbing to create leg loops.

Chest Harness

This simple and easy-to-tie chest harness is suitable for rigging a patient or yourself should you find that managing your

Fig. 4-35. Making a chest harness in the vertical world.

Fig. 4-36. Climber's cow's tail is clipped through her chest harness.

patient is easier when being kept upright by a chest harness. This chest harness is suitable in an improvised setting in which the patient will only rely on it for a short time.

Using a double-length sling:

1. Twist the sling (runner) so that a single X is formed in the center of the loop.
2. As if you were helping her into a jacket, insert your patient's arms (or your own) through each side of the loop; the X should lie in the center of her back.

3. Bring the two sides of the loop together with a carabiner. The carabiner should be located in the center of your patient's chest. Shorten the loop by adjusting the sling's knot so that the harness is relatively tight on the chest and will hold your patient upright.
4. Clip the climbing rope through the carabiner on the chest harness (no knot is necessary—the climbing rope should run freely through the carabiner). See fig. 4-35.

If you or your patient is connected to the rope via a cow's tail, simply clip the cow's tail through the chest harness' carabiner instead of the climbing rope. See fig. 4.36.

To add stability and support to this basic setup:

5. Use a short rescue loop to tie a Prusik hitch onto your patient's rope and clip the chest harness carabiner into the rescue loop. Slide the Prusik up

the rope until your patient feels more comfortable.

Head Sling

A head sling should not be rigged without some sort of chest harness included. You do not want the entire weight of the upper torso to be relying on the neck muscles to keep the body upwardly oriented.

1. Slip a runner behind your patient's head (pad the back of your patient's head if possible). Get creative! Adjust and tie cord and webbing to whatever you need to keep your patient's head upright. You can also use the waist of a shirt or pair of pants, or the opening of a bag. Slip it over the back of your patient's head and bring it together in front, securing it either with a carabiner poked through the material or with a knot.

2. How you attach your patient's head sling to the rope will depend on how your patient is rigged. If your patient is rigged on a cow's tail, you may be able to clip the head sling into the carabiner extended off the cow's tail. If the climbing rope is attached to your patient's waist, connect a runner or cordelette with a friction hitch to the rope and adjust accordingly once the head sling is clipped to that runner.

Lower Body and Foot Sling

The process for creating a lower body and foot sling for a patient is the same as described above for creating a head sling. The only difference from the head sling is the length of material you need for attaching the lower body/foot sling to the rope. Wrap whatever material is available around your patient's lower body or feet and bring the two sides together, connecting them with a carabiner or knot. You also have the option of girth-hitching something around the patient's quadriceps and/or feet to keep him in position. (In either case, but especially when girth-hitching, include padding.) Make sure that the sling is long enough so that you are not inadvertently causing your patient to tip backward.

SHORT ROPING

Short roping is a guiding technique that should only be employed by experienced professionals. Basically a short piece of rope is attached to a wobbly climber (e.g., who is hurt, disoriented, uncoordinated, etc.). The guide holds the rope so that if the climber slips the guide can pull quickly and definitively on the climber to stop any sort of slip or fall. The guide is generally about 3–5 feet from the wobbly climber and needs to be ultra attentive. Guides use the technique in exposed terrain where an unexpected fall would be bad. By tying to the climber, the guide is putting her life on the line if she is not able to support the climber in all the terrain they encounter. This technique might be useful to a rescuer when shepherding someone down a trail with a nasty drop on one side, but should not be used without practice and knowledge of the consequences of failure.

CHAPTER 5

Real-life improvised rescue on Ama Dablam in the Himalaya

Ascending

In this chapter we talk about ascending a fixed line, rope soloing and other handy ascension methods. A line is "fixed" when it is directly anchored above you (and possibly below you as well).

Fixed lines are also used in big-mountain climbing to protect exposed terrain that is not necessarily vertical. These lines are used much the same way as in vertical terrain, typically with both ends clipped to an anchor at the top and bottom, though commonly the climber can just clip to the line to back up his movement, not relying wholly on the line for upward progress.

In this chapter we focus on vertical or near vertical terrain. Let's begin with a look at some of the simplest means of ascending a rope and their applications for improvised self-rescue.

STUCK HANGING

Eventually, no matter how lucky you are, something will get caught in your rappel device, long hair or clothing being the most common. If you continue rappelling, whatever is caught will continue to get sucked up by your belay device, clogging it up, not to mention creating a great deal of pain if it happens to be your hair or skin getting reeled in.

No matter what the stuck object is, in order to continue rappelling, the rappel device must be unweighted—not too tricky if you are rappelling a low-angle route where you may be able to simply stand up on the rock to unweight the device. But what about on a free-hanging rappel?

Here is an easy fix to something stuck in your belay device:

1. Free your brake hand using a Munter-mule-overhand (MMO), leg wraps, or by engaging your third-hand backup.
2. Attach either a spare runner or a rescue loop onto the rope above your belay device using a friction hitch. (Take care not to push it too high above or you will be stuck with

GIRTH
HITCHED
SLINGS

Fig. 5-1. Using a chain of runners girth-hitched together and attached to the rope with a friction hitch, the climber is able to stand up and remove stuck items from her rappel device.

the problem of retrieving it.)

3. Now girth-hitch whatever kind of webbing or cordage you have available to the runner or rescue loop already attached to the rope. Keep girth-hitching runners together until you have the desired length for a foot loop.

4. Stand up in the foot loop, grabbing the rope *not* the friction hitch (fig. 5-1); if you grab the hitch it will slide down. You have successfully unweighted the rappel device and are in a position to effectively deal. If your hair or clothing is really stuck, you may have to rip it out; sometimes that's the only option.

5. Once you have remedied the situation, sink back down onto your rappel device. Undo the string of girth-hitched runners and reach up to remove the foot sling's friction hitch.

Climbers can get stuck in a similar predicament when using a Prusik hitch or klemheist placed above the rappel device as a back-up. If a climber does not adequately compensate for the amount of rope sliding through her belay device, while simultaneously moving the Prusik down the line above her, she may find herself suddenly stuck hanging from a fully weighted Prusik.

Here is an easy fix to the Prusik conundrum using a *foot wrap:*

1. With one hand tight on your two brake strands, use your other hand to run the rope under one foot and back up to a few feet above your belay device.

2. Holding tight to the four strands, step your foot into the loop and

stand up. This should allow you to loosen the Prusik wraps and slide the Prusik down to the rappel device. If necessary you can wrap the rope around your foot several times to create a more sturdy foot loop.

3. Slowly transition back into your rappelling position, taking care to retain your grip on the brake strands while sinking back down and then slowly undoing the foot wraps.

IMPROVISING AN ASCENSION RIG

This improvised fixed-line ascension rig is an easy, quick, and versatile way to get up a line without the use of mechanical ascenders. Times you may need to ascend a fixed line include:

■ Retrieving a stuck rappel line or if you have rappelled past an anchor.

■ Attending to a hurt leader.

■ Exiting a crevasse.

■ Getting back on route after falling on a traverse or off a large roof.

The rig is made from materials that a climber is typically already carrying on her rack: a rescue loop and a cordelette. These are used to make a waist loop and a foot loop (a waist Prusik and a foot Prusik). These lengths of material do not have to be reserved just for creating an ascension rig; these two pieces of cord can serve multiple purposes and do not need to remain hanging from your harness pre-tied.

There are many different ways of creating an ascension rig and the process for correctly sizing your rig varies depending on if you are using one foot loop, two foot loops, or a locking girth hitch on your heel. There is no right or wrong way; the bottom line is figuring out what lengths work best for you to allow you to move efficiently on the rope.

Below are the steps for tying a one-foot-loop ascension rig. This rig can be tied using a spare cordelette and provides a clip-in

THE KNIFE AS LAST RESORT

It is a good idea to get in the habit of carrying a small knife on your harness, particularly on longer climbs. Perhaps something is hopelessly stuck in your belay device, or the rope got hung up on a rappel and is irretrievable. You may want to cut up webbing to make an anchor or remove crispy, old webbing at a rappel station. Save the knife as a last resort if you are actually on the rope (e.g., your long hair is caught in the belay device). Look for other alternatives to getting unstuck such as the ones described in this chapter. Sharp knives can cut weighted, taut ropes in an instant. If you do use your knife, before opening it, attach webbing or cordage with a friction hitch onto the rope above you and clip in to it. That way should the knife mistakenly slip and slice the rope, you have a backup attachment to the climbing rope.

Fig. 5-2. Foot Prusik. Climber with a properly measured foot Prusik. The loop ("A") will be used for tying a Prusik hitch on the climbing rope.

point so you will have two points of attachment to the rope when ascending.

1. To tie a waist loop (waist Prusik), cut a piece of 7-millimeter cord as long as you are tall, plus 6 inches to a foot. Tie a double fisherman's or Flemish bend with the ends to form a loop.

2. For a foot loop (foot Prusik), cut a piece of 7-millimeter cord that is twice your height. On one end, tie an overhand on a bight that leaves a small loop big enough to clip a carabiner to. On the other end, tie a figure eight on a bight that leaves a 6- to 8-inch loop. Girth-hitch that loop to your foot. Clip the other end in to a locking carabiner on your belay loop.

3. Tie a figure eight on a bight that leaves a 10-inch loop. This knot should be about crotch level if your foot is on the ground and girth-hitched into the foot loop. The other strand, going to your harness carabiner, should be loose and 1 or 2 feet long. Proper length ensures you will achieve full extension as you push your foot Prusik up the rope. See fig. 5-2.

ASCENDING WITH AN ASCENSION RIG

The movement of ascension, when executed by an experienced climber, is impressive to watch. Some expert big-wall climbers are reputed to ascend with mechanical devices as quickly as they walk.

Here is a look at how to ascend with your newly tied ascension rig:

1. Attach your waist Prusik and your foot Prusik to the rope with Prusik hitches. The waist Prusik is tied farthest away from you, above the foot Prusik—think "waist away." (If using a Purcell Prusik, just substitute it for "foot Prusik" in these instructions.) Make sure you have secured the friction hitch around *both* strands of rope. And before being put to use, friction hitches need to be dressed and tested.

2. Clip the small loop on your foot Prusik and a section of your waist Prusik in to a locking carabiner clipped in to the belay loop on your harness (fig. 5-3). Note: If you will be passing a knot while ascending, each Prusik should be clipped into a separate carabiner (see chapter 7, Passing Knots).

3. Slide the waist Prusik up as high as you comfortably can reach.

4. Let your waist Prusik hold your weight as you tilt backward and slide your foot Prusik up as high as you can, ideally just below the base of your waist Prusik. Until you have significant rope weight beneath you, you will make your job of ascending easier by grabbing the rope with one hand below your Prusik and holding the rope steady with a downward pull as you move the Prusik up the line.

5. Bring your feet in under your butt and grab the climbing rope as high up as you can.

6. Stand up in your foot loop while pulling your torso up, using the rope for assistance.

7. Once steady—you are weighting the foot Prusik—push the waist Prusik up as high as you can. (You can keep using the rope for assistance.)

8. Now sink back down onto the waist Prusik and repeat the process. Again, again, again, and again. We call this "ascending" or "Prusiking."

Fig. 5-3. Ascension rig. "A" indicates the climber's waist Prusik; "B" indicates the climber's foot Prusik. Both are attached to the climber with locking carabiners clipped onto the climber's belay loop. Note the raised foot girth-hitched into the foot loop.

IMPROVISE: ASCENDING WITH A GARDA HITCH

What can you do if you are stuck needing to ascend a line but do not have much extra gear? You need to ascend to a fallen leader, for example. Combined with a long sling (or a few shorter slings girth-hitched together), the Garda hitch provides a way to ascend a line in a pinch (see fig. 5-4).

Use the climbing rope to tie a Garda hitch through two carabiners clipped into your belay loop. (Make sure to correctly tie the Garda so that slack can be pulled through correctly in relation to the direction of ascent.) Now set a friction hitch above the Garda on the climbing rope. Add as many slings as you need to create a foot loop to stand in. Stand up in your foot loop and pull as much slack as possible in through the Garda. Note: when ascending with a Garda hitch the foot Prusik is above the waist Prusik (the Garda). Now weight the Garda and push up your foot loop. Continue ascending in this manner.

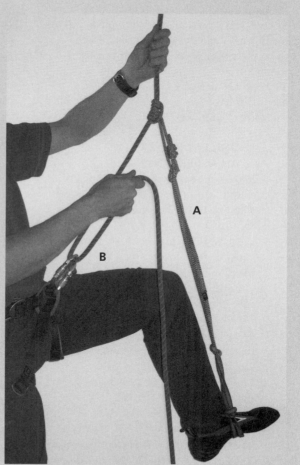

Fig. 5-4. Garda ascension rig. This rig is set up opposite of the Prusik ascension rig. "A" indicates the foot loop built out of girth-hitched slings and attached to the rope with a friction hitch. "B" indicates the Garda hitch tied off on the climber's belay loop with two carabiners. The climber is pulling on rope in his right hand to bring in slack through the Garda.

If you encounter pieces of gear while ascending simply clip your Prusiks through the runner's carabiner; similar to clipping through on a piece of protection while *simul-climbing*. There is no need to take your ascension rig off the rope.

Remember, as discussed in chapter 2, Rescue Knots, you may need to push the lower lip (or mouth) of the Prusik hitch open with your thumb in order to loosen it enough so that it will slide up the rope. You can also use other friction hitches to ascend; see the sidebar, "Improvise: Ascending with a Garda Hitch."

DESCENDING WITH AN ASCENSION RIG

Just as competent downclimbing is a skill stressed in rock climbing, the ability to descend a line is an important aspect of *fixed-line ascension.*

To descend using an ascension rig simply reverse the ascension process:

1. Stand up in your foot loop and slide your unweighted waist Prusik down the rope to the top of your foot Prusik. Leave an inch or two of space between the foot and waist Prusiks, or your waist Prusik will not grab as well when you sink onto it.
2. Now weight the waist Prusik and slide the unweighted foot Prusik down the line. Take care to not slide the foot Prusik down too far. You need to stand in the foot Prusik to unweight the waist Prusik; if you slid the foot Prusik down too far, you will not be able to reach it.
3. Repeat until you are back down.

MECHANICAL ASCENDERS

Ascenders made by Gibbs, Petzl, Blue-Water Ropes (Jumars), and so on are all types of mechanical ascenders that can be used for moving up and down fixed lines. Compared to friction hitches, mechanical ascenders have several advantages: they are extremely easy to clip on and off the rope, they slide with great ease, and they offer a comfortable grip.

There are, however, disadvantages to using mechanical ascenders: they are heavy, expensive, and their application is more limited than a set of Prusiks. Mechanical ascenders, if used at all, should be used with *great* caution when belaying or hauling. Testing shows that a shock load on mechanical ascenders can dangerously damage the rope—even shred the core. Because of mechanical ascenders' small camming area, in the event of a fall the rope can be severely damaged at as little as a third of the rope's rated strength. We do not recommend using a mechanical ascender in a raising system.

There are a few ascenders that are light and small. The Wild Country Ropeman and the Petzl Tibloc are two examples. These devices solve the weight issue while being quick and easy to use. They still have the disadvantage of being able to severely damage (even cut) the rope in a dynamic loading event, and they are not releasable under a load. Prusik hitches are the rescue tool of choice despite the apparent advantage of a piece of manufactured gear and easy application.

ASCENDING WITH MECHANICAL ASCENDERS

Refer to the instructions that come with your mechanical ascenders for proper use. Some amount of practice is needed to develop smooth technique. Take the time to learn how to do it right.

To link yourself to the ascender, girth-hitch a runner or a daisy chain through your harness, then clip this with a locking carabiner into the eyehole on the lower section of the ascender.

If using a mechanical ascender on a traverse, clip a nonlocking carabiner through the eyehole of the ascender and then to the rope. Should your ascender come off the rope (traversing is the most likely scenario during which that can happen), you will still be attached to the rope with a carabiner.

DESCENDING WITH MECHANICAL ASCENDERS

Descending with mechanical ascenders is a little trickier than with an ascension rig; they are called ascenders for a reason! They like to go up, not down. Use your thumb to release the camming unit while

Fig. 5-5. Clipping i...pped a figure eight on a bight...s a backup while she ascen...(top cord) and the foot...n the line.

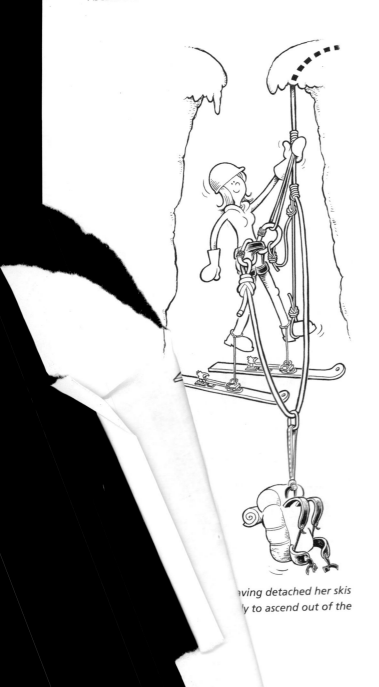

...aving detached her skis ...y to ascend out of the...

simultaneously sliding the ascender down the line. Do your best to avoid the start-and-stop jerk of the teeth biting down by keeping the ascender in line with the rope and pulling out slightly.

If descending on lower-angle terrain, orient the ascender on the rope as if you were going to ascend. But instead of going up, retract the camming unit and slide the ascender down the line as you descend. Clipping a nonlocking carabiner through the ascender's top eyehole and the rope can help keep the ascender attached to the rope while you disengage the camming unit.

Make sure to practice in a controlled setting (on the ground or with a belay) before lifting off.

GLACIERS

In essence, the process of ascending out of a crevasse is exactly the same as ascending a fixed line in the desert. There are, of course, a few added steps pertinent to the unique environment of a crevasse's innards; these are addressed in detail in specific glacier-travel books (like Andy Tyson's *Glacier Mountaineering*).

If you have fallen into a crevasse, take a look around behind you, below you, and in front of you. It is easy to develop tunnel vision in stressful situations and there may be a simple solution right in front of your eyes. Maybe with the use of your ice ax you can easily climb out. Are the walls of the crevasse close enough together that you could stem your way out? You can

CLIPPING IN SHORT

Whenever ascending or descending a line, if the line is not weighted or fixed, it is a good habit to tie a figure eight on a bight every 10 feet or so and clip that bight into a spare locking carabiner on your belay loop. In the event that something should fail, you have created a trustworthy, relatively close backup for yourself. A fall of just a few feet is obviously preferable to falling the length of the rope back to your original tie-in point. This is sometimes called "tying in short" (see fig. 5-5).

ASCENDING WITH MECHANICAL ASCENDERS

Refer to the instructions that come with your mechanical ascenders for proper use. Some amount of practice is needed to develop smooth technique. Take the time to learn how to do it right.

To link yourself to the ascender, girth-hitch a runner or a daisy chain through your harness, then clip this with a locking carabiner into the eyehole on the lower section of the ascender.

If using a mechanical ascender on a traverse, clip a nonlocking carabiner through the eyehole of the ascender and then to the rope. Should your ascender come off the rope (traversing is the most likely scenario during which that can happen), you will still be attached to the rope with a carabiner.

DESCENDING WITH MECHANICAL ASCENDERS

Descending with mechanical ascenders is a little trickier than with an ascension rig; they are called ascenders for a reason! They like to go up, not down. Use your thumb to release the camming unit while

Fig. 5-5. Clipping in short. Climber has clipped a figure eight on a bight back in to her harness as a backup while she ascends. Note the waist Prusik (top cord) and the foot Prusik (bottom cord) tied on the line.

Fig. 5-6. A climber having detached her skis and backpack, is ready to ascend out of the crevasse.

simultaneously sliding the ascender down the line. Do your best to avoid the start-and-stop jerk of the teeth biting down by keeping the ascender in line with the rope and pulling out slightly.

If descending on lower-angle terrain, orient the ascender on the rope as if you were going to ascend. But instead of going up, retract the camming unit and slide the ascender down the line as you descend. Clipping a nonlocking carabiner through the ascender's top eyehole and the rope can help keep the ascender attached to the rope while you disengage the camming unit.

Make sure to practice in a controlled setting (on the ground or with a belay) before lifting off.

GLACIERS

In essence, the process of ascending out of a crevasse is exactly the same as ascending a fixed line in the desert. There are, of course, a few added steps pertinent to the unique environment of a crevasse's innards; these are addressed in detail in specific glacier-travel books (like Andy Tyson's *Glacier Mountaineering*).

If you have fallen into a crevasse, take a look around behind you, below you, and in front of you. It is easy to develop tunnel vision in stressful situations and there may be a simple solution right in front of your eyes. Maybe with the use of your ice ax you can easily climb out. Are the walls of the crevasse close enough together that you could stem your way out? You can always try and call up to a teammate to ask her to send down some equipment like another ice ax. If the crevasse's bottom is within sight, another option is to have your partners lower you; you may be able to simply walk out the bottom of the crevasse or move down to a better spot for climbing out. However, watch out that you are gently lowered onto the crevasse floor—it may be just another unstable snow bridge like the one you fell through in the first place. Move with care and stay on belay.

Depending on your mode of travel (boots, snowshoes, or skis), it may be necessary to drop your skis or snowshoes either to climb or ascend. Unhook them and let them dangle from their leashes (see fig. 5-6), or stow them on your pack.

USING AN ASCENSION RIG

If you can't find any other way out and you are uninjured, then it is time to ascend. Some specifics, like your pack tether, chest harness, and your particular ascension rig may differ depending on the setup you're using.

1. Unhook your pack's waist belt and sternum strap and *gently* load your pack onto the rope. Hastily dropping your pack only shocks the system (which may still be your partner holding your fall). The pack hanging below you will act as a weight holding the rope in place, making ascension easier (the same reason why aid climbers often ascend the line from which the haul bag hangs).
2. Unclip the rope from your chest harness.

Fig. 5-7. A climber negotiates past a crevasse lip while ascending.

3. Insert your feet into the foot loops. There is no need to tie your ascension rig onto the rope—in glacier travel it should already be in place.
4. Yell "Ascending" up to your teammates and start making your way up the line.

Use your body and feet to keep yourself off the wall if the wall is less than vertical. You want to keep the Prusik hitch as free of snow as possible. Snow caught in your Prusik will only make your job more difficult, as snowy, wet Prusiks are more difficult to slide up the line and do not catch as well.

The lip of the crevasse is usually the worst part of this process (see fig. 5-7). Often, as a climber falls, the climbing rope slices downward into the lip of the crevasse. The rope can be so deeply entrenched that the remaining team members above must send down a separate line and the climber must switch over, retying into the new line.

In the best of circumstances, your partners will pad the lip of the crevasse with an ice ax shaft or backpack. This way, as you approach the lip your weight on the line does not cause the rope to continue cutting into the snow deeper and deeper. As you approach the lip, batten down the hatches: pull up and tighten your hood, zip up everything, make sure snow can't slide down your sleeves, neck, or waistband.

Here are a few tips and tricks for passing the crevasse lip:

- Do not hesitate to use your ice ax to gain purchase in your upward push. If the snow is particularly soft, use the ice ax's shaft instead of the pick.
- Get aggressive with your feet, kicking footholds for purchase in your upward fight.
- Be wary that Prusiks can be a bit slower to catch once wet and choked with snow. You can minimize this clogging by trying to place your hand under the Prusik, protecting it as you move it up the rope through the snow.
- If possible have one of your teammates toss you a line (either excess rope, a long strand of webbing, or a cordelette). This should be either attached to the

anchor, or your partner can simply hold it as long as she is securely attached to either the anchor or the haul line and is in a secure position (butt and boots dug into the snow). Pull on the cord to help you with the final few feet. (Because your Prusik would take the weight of any slip you might take while ascending these last feet, this improvisational, hand-over-hand aid from your partner is acceptable.)

USING MECHANICAL ASCENDERS ON GLACIERS

Some people opt to use mechanical ascenders for their waist Prusik while crossing glaciers. Mechanical ascenders can easily be placed on and taken off the rope, an advantage if you are using fixed lines while on glaciated terrain.

But because of their camming action, mechanical ascenders should not be placed on a rope while traveling. As discussed above, the cam can severely damage the rope in a dynamic fall. Instead, mechanical ascenders should be kept clipped off to the side on a harness. Only after the fall should the ascender be placed on a rope.

Like the Prusik hitch, a mechanical ascender can get jammed with snow while ascending out of a crevasse. Be wary of the ascender's tendency to slip back down when placed on icy, snowy ropes. You must pull directly down on the ascender to achieve optimal bite on the rope, a sometimes difficult step when ascending through the less than vertical angle of a crevasse's lip.

PRACTICE: FIXED-LINE ASCENSION

Fixed-line ascension is easy to practice either by yourself or with a partner. Remember how slowly it goes on your first shot, then imagine having tried it for your first time hanging below the surface of an icy crevasse. You will be glad you practiced.

1. Fix a line to a solid anchor built off a tree or balcony, etc. To make it worth your efforts, aim to hang the line about 20 feet off the ground.
2. Now attach your ascension rig to the rope and start ascending. When you reach the top, descend back down.

If you have a partner, rather than fixing a line, create a top-rope anchor:

1. Have your partner put you on belay as if you were going to top-rope a climb, and attach your ascension rig to your side of the rope.
2. As you ascend, your partner belays slack through the system, providing you with at least half a rope length of fun ascending or torture (depending on how you look at it).

ASCENDING TO A HURT LEADER

If you are unable to lower your leader back down to the anchor (as discussed in chapter 4, Descending) and she is unable to assist herself, you will need to ascend to her.

With One Rope

1. If possible, have her reinforce the piece she is hanging on. (Do not rule out the possibility of her creating an anchor, attaching herself to it, and fixing her end of the lead rope to the anchor.)
2. Examine your anchor carefully. Depending on the anchor's primary direction of pull you may need to add more (or reorient) pieces for the predominately upward pull of your fallen leader. Do your best! (See the chapter 3 sidebar, "Do You Need to Beef Up the Anchor?" for more thoughts on this.)
3. Escape the belay. By fixing the rope to the anchor you create a backup for yourself should (in a worst-case scenario) your partner's pieces fail while you are ascending.
4. If you plan on climbing while using the lead line only as a backup, use two waist-sized loops attached to the lead line with friction hitches. Use good movement on the rock as your primary means of protection while pushing your Prusiks ahead as you ascend. In some instances (e.g., if the rock is extremely overhanging), you may have to ascend the line with an ascension rig (described earlier in this chapter).

5. As you ascend you may want to remove some of the gear your partner placed, freeing it for use above. On the other hand, because you and your partner are relying on only the top piece of gear, additional pieces are your backup should the top piece fail—so leave a few of the lead pieces in as you ascend. Every situation will demand a different solution.

6. Once you reach your partner, build a new anchor. Transfer both her and the rope to the anchor.

7. Depending on what your next steps are you will need to descend to free the bottom end of the climbing rope if it is fixed. How you choose to do so (e.g. single- or double-strand rappel or descending with your Prusik) will depend on the specific circumstances.

With More Than One Rope

The advantage of utilizing two ropes while ascending to an injured leader is that you are relying on two independent systems; one backs up the other.

1–4. Follow steps 1 through 4 for ascending with one rope.

5. Set up a new multidirectional anchor for upward pull (if you can).

6. Attach the top of the second rope to the new anchor and tie in to the bottom end.

7. Rope-solo (free or aid) up the route using the second line as the belay (see later in this chapter for a description of rope soloing). Clip your lead-line through the pieces of gear placed by the leader.

ROPE SOLOING

Climbing by yourself with a backup rope system is called *rope soloing*. Some climbers complete many climbs this way—everything from big-wall to small-crag climbs. It is possible to solo free climb and solo aid climb with a self-belay.

Times when you might choose to rope solo or rope solo aid in an improvised rescue scenario include climbing up to:

■ Assist an injured leader.

■ Retrieve a stuck rappel rope.

■ Assist a partner who has become so incapacitated that he cannot belay you and the only way out is up. Rope soloing the pitch may be your best option.

The best way to rope solo is with a special device that allows the rope to feed through while you climb, but that locks if you fall (manufacturers of the Petzl GriGri and Trango Cinch do not recommend these devices for solo aiding though some people use them).

There are specific devices that work much better for rope soloing than what is described here. But, in keeping with the improvised character of self-rescue, we will assume you do not have such devices with you. The main challenge is to move up terrain that you feel comfortable on, staying protected by the rope despite there not being a second person belaying you.

These are acceptable systems. There *is* the possibility of longer falls if you have just put some slack into your rope backup system. A rescue is not the time to learn these systems, however—it is best to

practice before you are in the heat of the moment.

Rope Soloing, Basic Method

These systems can be used for rope-solo free climbing and rope-solo aid climbing. (Aiding refers to relying on gear placements rather than climbing movement to move up a rock face. See "French-Freeing" at the end of this chapter for more information on aid climbing.)

1. Attach the top end of the rope to a multidirectional anchor. This anchor should mainly protect for an upward pull.
2. Tie in to the other end of the rope (the bottom end of the rope stack).
3. From the anchor (the top of the rope stack), pull out enough rope to climb about 10 feet. Tie a bow line on a bight through your belay loop and clip the bight's tail off with a locking carabiner. (Alternately, you can tie a figure eight on a bight and clip it to two locking carabiners on your belay loop; we refer to this as your "short tie-in".)

Fig. 5-8. *An overview of rope-soloing up to an injured leader. The rescuer has created a separate anchor and is using a second rope to ascend to the patient. (**Note:** Because of the potential shifting of the anchor that may occur while rope-soloing, it is very important that the rescuer has constructed a multidirectional anchor. This can be accomplished by placing multidirectional pieces or better yet by maintaining the anchor's direction of pull with a friction hitch tied around the climbing rope and attached to a separate piece of gear placed above the anchor. The taut friction hitch will hold the anchor in its intended direction of pull, minimizing shifting of gear while the rescuer climbs or shock loading should the rescuer fall.) The top of the rope stack is fixed to the anchor and the rescuer is tied in just a few yards away. As he ascends the rescuer adjusts his tie-in point to maintain an upward pull on the bottom anchor. The rescuer is also tied in to the bottom end of the rope (indicated by the outside line of rope between the rope stack and the rescuer).*

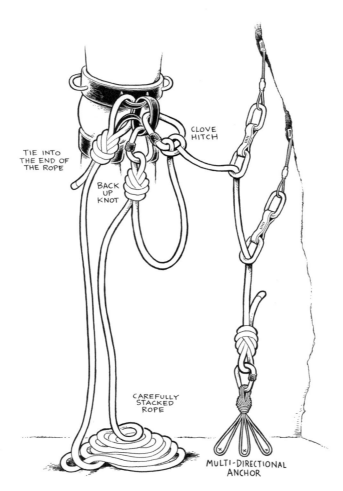

CLOVE
HITCH

TIE INTO
THE END OF
THE ROPE

BACK
UP
KNOT

CAREFULLY
STACKED
ROPE

MULTI-DIRECTIONAL
ANCHOR

*Fig. 5-9. An up-close look at rope soloing using a clove hitch as an adjustable clip-in point. The figure eight on a bight clipped to the belay loop with a locking carabiner serves as a backup to the clove hitch. (Approximately ten feet is a manageable amount of slack to maintain between the two knots.) As the climber ascends, these lengths will need to be adjusted periodically. Note how the climber is tied into the bottom end of the rope with a figure eight follow-through, while the top end of the rope is fixed to the anchor. **Note:** Because of the potential shifting of the anchor that may occur while rope-soloing, it is very important that the rescuer has constructed a multidirectional anchor. This can be accomplished by placing multidirectional pieces or better yet by maintaining the anchor's direction of pull with a friction hitch tied around the climbing rope and attached to a separate piece of gear placed above the anchor. The taut friction hitch will hold the anchor in its intended direction of pull, minimizing shifting of gear while the rescuer climbs or shock loading should the rescuer fall.*

4. Climb up about 5 feet and place a piece at your chest (or clip into your fallen leader's piece of gear). Clip in the rope between you and the anchor. You will have to experiment with distances, though you should not need to adjust your tie-in to let you continue climbing higher. Retie in so that you have 10 to 20 more feet of rope to climb with, and protect as necessary. (See fig. 5-8.)

Keep in mind:

■ Throughout this process you need to remain tied in the whole time.

■ When you retie in, tie your new knot first and then untie your old one.

■ Remember that the slack from untying the old tie-in will add to the distance you can travel (or fall!).

■ It is best not to have to retie in between protection placements.

■ With this method, you are climbing with slack in the system and any fall will be as big as the slack you put in the system.

■ Watch out for making ground or ledge falls possible by adding too much slack.

■ Clip in short as a backup whenever possible.

■ Move your leader's pieces of gear or *leap-frog* as necessary as you climb.

Rope Soloing, Alternate Method

High on a wall, where ground or ledge falls are not possible, there is a variation to the basic rope-soloing method. Since you may not hit anything if your short tie-in knot slips, you can use a clove hitch, which is easier to adjust but is less secure than a bowline or a figure eight.

1. After securing the top end of the rope to a multidirectional anchor, tie in to the other end (or measure off the distance you ultimately want to climb and tie in to the rope there).

2. Put a locking carabiner on your belay loop.

3. From the anchor, take enough rope to climb a bit, and then attach a clove hitch to your locker at that point.

4. Climb and protect as necessary, while adjusting rope through your clove hitch to allow further progress. The clove hitch is backed up by the tie-in you have at the end of the rope. Careful! Clove hitches need to be cinched down in order to work. Your movement during climbing can easily loosen a hitch. Make sure to set the clove hitch well and that you have a good backup knot.

These two methods can be combined: tie in using a bowline with 30 feet of slack in the system and then use a clove hitch to reduce the slack as you climb. The important thing is that the climbing should be relatively easy for you to consider using this technique, and you should try to estimate distances so that you do not have to fiddle with your knots during a tricky move.

FRENCH-FREEING

French-free is a term used by some U.S. climbers. Generally, when freeing a route you do not use your protection pieces for hand- or footholds. If you do, it is called "using a point of aid" or "French-freeing"

Fig. 5-10. French-freeing. To help himself through a difficult section, the climber grabs on a piece of gear that he may or may not clip the lead rope through. He could also extend the piece of gear with a long sling for stepping up, in order to gain as much height as possible for his next placement.

(fig. 5-10). Without getting into the etymology or politics of the phrase, it is a good technique to employ if faced with a tough move, or if you are in a situation that you need to move quickly though and do not have time to work out the crux sequence. If a thunderstorm is impending and you are leading a tough pitch, you might want to speed it up with some selective gear grabbing.

- Clip a quickdraw to the bolt and grab the draw while clipping the rope; keep climbing.
- Place a piece and pull on it to get up to the next good handhold.
- Add a foot sling to a piece for a high reach. Free climbers generally regard this as poor style. But getting yourself out of trouble is very good style, so yard away—just don't say you freed the route.

SIMUL-CLIMBING

Simul-climbing (sometimes referred to as a "running belay system") is a great technique that allows competent climbers to cover easy but exposed terrain quickly while maintaining some backup protection from a rope system. A common use of simul-climbing is on steep snow slopes. The team is roped together and all moving up the slope. The leader places protection and clips the rope through to it. The followers clip through, or if a climber is last on the rope he may clean the protection. This is a basic simul-climbing system.

On rock there are usually not more than two people on the rope, one tied to each end. The leader places protection and the follower takes it out when she gets to it. They should always have a few pieces of protection on the line between them. If either climber falls, he will probably pull the other off. Although the consequences would be greater had they not had a rope in the first place, falling while simul-climbing can still result in serious injury. The consequences of a fall necessitate the rope system, though the simul-climbing system is meant for speed over safety. Climbers should use it with caution: the terrain should be well within their abilities, the system protecting against the unlikely event of a fall. Climbers should not travel in exposed terrain roped together with no protection between them. Many climbers have died in serious accidents when traveling roped on steep slopes but without the use of protection.

If trouble arises while simul-climbing, the rescue procedures will be the same as in other situations. The climber at either end of the rope faces the potential of needing to build an anchor if there is trouble at the other end. For this reason it is always good for both climbers to have some gear and slings, just in case.

HELPING YOUR PARTNER AID THROUGH THE CRUX

If you anticipate your partner is going to have a difficult time with a route's crux, do not be shy about placing a piece of aid for him above the difficult move. Extend the piece's runner so that when your partner is right below the crux he will be able to reach the runner and pull on it; you can even build him a little etrier if need be. (This runner is not necessarily what you want to clip your lead rope in to. Use a runner of appropriate length for that.) Once past the difficult section, your partner can clean the protection. This trick can save precious time and energy on both ends of the rope.

CHAPTER 6

The only way out is up!

Raising

Raising a climber is never physically easy, but with practice a raising system is not necessarily tough to build. Some raising systems are quite complex, but we will start with simple systems and work our way up. All of the systems are described with the rescuer above the climber, and all systems are described using carabiners as the pulley mechanism.

Times you might want to raise a climber include:

- Giving a quick assist to your second through a short, tough section of the climb.
- Raising one pitch or less in order for a hurt, tired, wet climber to top out the climb.
- When using a crevasse rescue system (to get your partner back to the surface).
- During a multipitch rescue for an injured climber, where it is not possible to descend.

A quick and helpful solution to a difficult crux section is to keep a tight belay, which may need to become more of a downright fish fight. The 1:1 pull is definitely effective, and all climbers (and certainly guides) have used it successfully. With good positioning, the lift can happen with the legs. Lock your belay device off while lifting, and then pull in captured rope while the climber fights to maintain his position. This method will not work if the climber can't assist while the belayer captures rope through the belay device.

With the climber above on a top-rope or through a redirect, it is possible to do a counterweight pull by locking your belay device and dropping to a crouch. Then, because of the friction at the top-rope carabiners, it is generally possible to quickly stand up and take in rope at the same time, locking off when standing again. Repeat this sequence. If you need to see this in action, head to the nearest super rad sport-climbing area. There should be plenty of folks using this technique to "work" routes.

DROP-LINE ASSIST 1:1

This next simple system is great for a short hard crux that leads to easier ground. It is not possible to do a drop-line assist if the climber is more than one-third the rope length from the rescuer/belayer. With a second rope you can do this assist with the climber a full pitch away.

Make sure the standing end of the rope is anchored to the master point (MP) (often it already is, if you are clipped in with a figure eight on a bight or clove hitch). Lower the rope stack to the climber. She can now use the rope to pull on as you belay her in. She gets to do the hard work! If she is adept at friction hitches, she can get busy and throw one on the spare line as well, pushing it up the rope as she ascends. You might also want to pre-tie loops before you throw the rope, so she has something to pull on. Simple is good!

DROP A LOOP 2:1

It is possible to convert a drop-line assist to a simple 2:1 pulley assist. However, the farthest the climber can be from you is about 75 feet (if you have two 160-foot ropes), or about 50 feet (if you have only one 160-foot rope).

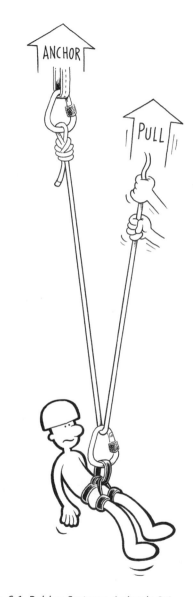

Fig. 6-1. Raising Systems. A simple 2:1

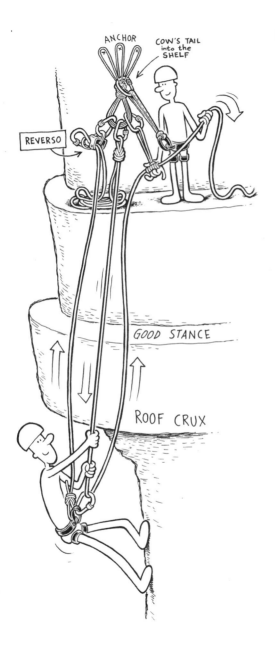

ANCHOR

COW'S TAIL
into the
SHELF

REVERSO

GOOD STANCE

ROOF CRUX

1. Get hands-free: you will need your hands free of the belay for pulling.
2. Doublecheck that the standing end of the rope is attached to the anchor.
3. Clip a carabiner onto the rope stack. The carabiner should slide freely on the rope; do not tie it onto the rope in any way. Drop this rope and carabiner to the climber. Keep hold of the other end of the rope.
4. Have the climber take the carabiner and clip it in to his belay loop.
5. Now you can pull on the unanchored end of the rope you just dropped him. The climber can help by trying to pull on the anchored end of the rope. He should slowly go up.

Caution! The climber is tied off to the belay at his starting height. So if you let go he will drop back down to the tie-off point. For a quick short-aid section, it might be fine to hand-haul. For a longer pull use a Prusik to take in slack or put a locking carabiner with a Munter on the MP or shelf. As you pull up, take in the slack through the Munter. In cases of a long haul (e.g., the rest of the pitch), it would be best to completely escape the belay (since you will not be resuming it).

This 2:1 can also be used in crevasse rescue. It is a good way to get the climber out of a crevasse that has a nasty lip above the climber's original line.

Fig. 6-2. Raising Systems. A drop loop assist is an easy way to create a 2:1.

3:1 SYSTEMS

A 3:1 raising system is a good way to get a climber up a short section without dropping a rope to him. There are a number of variations to building a 3:1: it can be built on the anchor, with a self-blocking belay device, with a Garda hitch, off your harness, and as a complex 3:1 (aka the *Spanish Burton*), which allows for pulling in a downward direction.

It is best to do long raises off the anchor (as opposed to off your harness). If you are building a system specifically to raise someone, there are several things you can do to help yourself out:

■ Build the anchor high, mainly so the rope runs cleanly over the edge of the ledge you might be on, but also so you have some room to work.

■ If you have pulleys, use them instead of carabiners—one attached to the pulley-point Prusik and one at the anchor pulley.

■ Create a *self-tending ratchet Prusik* by putting a belay device (like an ATC) on the loaded line running through the anchor. The ATC will not provide friction, though it will block the ratchet Prusik from flipping through the carabiner through which the climbing rope runs (or from getting sucked up by the anchor pulley if you are not using a specialized Prusik-minding pulley). Creating a self-tending ratchet Prusik saves you the effort of resetting the ratchet and maintaining it. If you do not have a belay device to insert here, you will need to watch the ratchet very carefully.

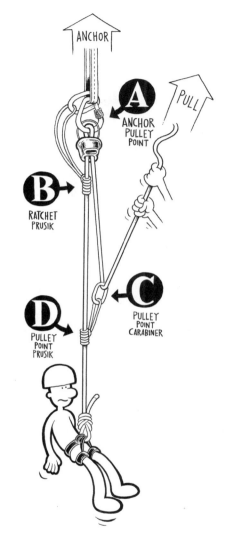

Fig. 6-3. Raising Systems. A simple 3:1. "A" indicates the anchor pulley point, "B" the ratchet Prusik; "C" the pulley point carabiner, and "D" the pulley point Prusik.

3:1 OFF THE ANCHOR

1. If belaying off the anchor, get hands-free. If belaying off your body, escape the belay.

2. Take a rescue loop and tie a Prusik onto the weighted belay strand. Clip the loop into a locking carabiner on the master point or shelf. (This is the ratchet Prusik.)

3. Take another rescue loop and reach forward, down the loaded strand leading to your climber, as far as you can and attach the rescue loop with a Prusik hitch at that point on the line—a "pulley point." (A rescue loop tied in this manner is the pulley-point Prusik.)

4. Clip a locking carabiner to this pulley-point Prusik and then clip the loose brake strand through the carabiner. (If carrying a pulley, use it here instead of a locking carabiner.) Maintain a hand on the brake strand while you complete the remaining steps.

5. If an ATC is available, use it to create a self-tending ratchet. Attach it to the brake strand as close as possible to where the rope exits the Munter-mule-overhand (MMO). Clip a locking carabiner around the rope and through the belay device and attach it to the MP. (This locking carabiner is the anchor pulley.)

6. Transfer the load onto the ratchet Prusik by slowly undoing the mule-overhand and the Munter. Remove the carabiner on which the MMO was tied. Pull in all slack.

Fig. 6-4. A 3:1 raising system with self-blocking belay device. "A" indicates the self-blocking belay device (which replaces the need for a ratchet Prusik); "B" the load strand; "C" the pulley point Prusik; "D" the haul strand.

7. Once you have removed all slack created by undoing the MMO, you are now ready to haul. As you pull in line you may need to "set" the ratchet by pushing it forward before easing off your pulling. Eventually the pulley-point Prusik will reach your belay device. At this point you will need to reset it.

8. To reset the pulley-point Prusik, ease off the line, letting the ratchet hold the climber's weight, and then push the pulley-point Prusik as far forward as you can. Repeat as necessary.

3:1 WITH SELF-BLOCKING OR LOCKING-ASSIST BELAY DEVICE

If belaying off the anchor with a self-blocking or *locking-assist belay device,* there is no need to set a ratchet Prusik. Simply follow steps 3 and 4 above in "3:1 Off the Anchor." Eventually you will have to reset the pulley-point Prusik, following step 7. Fig. 6-4 shows a 3:1 system with a self-blocking device.

3:1 WITH A GARDA HITCH

Some climbers choose to build a 3:1 with a Garda hitch. This eliminates the need for a ratchet (and ratchet tending). It is fast and easy to set. One major downfall, however, is that this system is not easily reversible.

Fig. 6-5. A 3:1 employing the use of a Garda hitch. Note how the Garda is tied; the loop (see "Tying a Garda, step 3" in chapter 2) is clipped into the carabiner that corresponds to the side of the rope that you want holding the load.

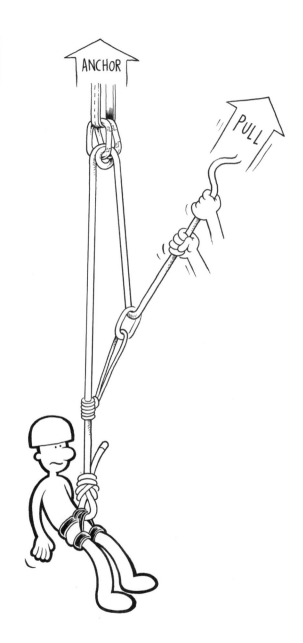

1. If belaying off your body, escape the belay, but instead of tying a MMO on the MP with the climbing rope, tie a Garda. If belaying off the anchor with a Munter, attach two nonlocking carabiners to the MP or shelf on the same side of the brake strand. While carefully maintaining your brake hand, tie a Garda hitch.
2. Pick up at steps 3 and 4 described above in "3:1 Off the Anchor." Take great care to maintain a hand on the brake strand while you do this.
3. Pull in the excess slack and undo the Munter hitch, removing the carabiner that the Munter was tied to.

Eventually you will need to reset, picking up as described in step 7 of "3:1 Off the Anchor."

3:1 OFF YOUR HARNESS

This system can also be set up off your harness when belaying off your body with a belay device. Instead of escaping the belay, get hands-free and pick up at step 2 described above in "3:1 Off the Anchor." (You can skip step 5, assuming your belay device is already part of the system).

Because the climber's weight is entirely on you (and then some, because of the pulley effect that multiplies forces), a 3:1 off your harness may be uncomfortable and will certainly hinder your range of motion,

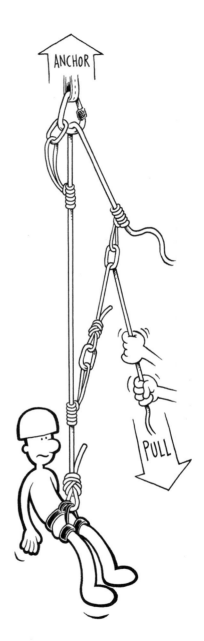

Fig. 6-6. The Spanish Burton is a complex 3:1 configured so that the rescuer may pull downward instead of up.

A 3:1 in action

restricting your ability to put your weight into the pull. But if you are concerned about trusting your anchor with the forces of hauling, if you need to haul your partner just a short distance, or if you want a speedy solution (no belay escapes with this one!), it is a viable option. Make sure you are in a secure position and the system is backed up on the anchor.

COMPLEX 3:1 SPANISH BURTON

A Spanish Burton puts gravity on your side with a downward pull. This is a big advantage if you are trying to raise someone significantly heavier than you up a vertical face.

1–3. Follow steps 1–3 described above in "3:1 Off the Anchor."

4. Attach a cordelette (or runner) to the rescue loop you just placed on the load strand in step 3.

5. Attach a rescue loop to the brake strand with a Prusik hitch. The rescue loop and carabiner (or pulley) coming off this Prusik will be your pulley-point Prusik.

6. Clip the cordelette (or runner) introduced in step 4 through the pulley-point Prusik. This cordelette is what you will pull on.

7. Pick up at step 5 described above in "3:1 Off the Anchor," and continue with the remaining steps.

135

PULLEY VERSUS CARABINER EFFICIENCY

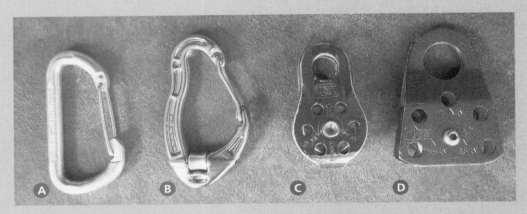

Fig. 6-7. (A) A wire-gate carabiner, (B) A DMM Revolver carabiner, which incorporates a small pulley into the carabiner's base, (C) A basic climbing pulley, and (D) A Prusik-minding pulley.

When a rope runs over or around something, there is friction. The more pronounced the angle of contact, the rougher the surface, and the more weight against the surface, the more the friction. If a rope holding 100 pounds were to run over a surface with an efficiency loss due to friction of 50 percent, you would need to double your effort and pull with 200 pounds of force in order to raise the load. Friction is our enemy in mechanical advantage systems. It makes us work harder and it puts higher forces on our gear than if we were working in a frictionless world. Different combinations of ropes and carabiners, along with the actual forces in play, will result in different friction coefficients.

Below we list efficiencies for carabiners and pulleys. This is intended for general information purposes and does not apply to all situations or all combinations of gear.

Oval carabiner: 70 percent
Basic climbing pulley: 80–85 percent
DMM's Revolver: 75–80 percent
High-quality rescue pulley: 90+ percent

What efficiency percentages mean: If a carabiner has 70 percent efficiency and we are raising 100 pounds with it on a 2:1 system, we will have to lift with 59 pounds (not getting into static friction coefficients and rope-stretch details). If we are using a 3:1 system and there are two carabiners in the system, we will have to pull with 46 pounds—far from the 33.3 pounds of the frictionless world!

Note the diminishing returns as well. The more carabiners we add to the system, the smaller the gain. The forces on our gear keep going up, but we get less out of the system because the inefficiencies add up. Interestingly, when we stack a 3:1 on a 3:1 using carabiners to build the system, we need to input 21 pounds to lift 100. If instead we stack a 2:1 on a 3:1, we need to input 27 pounds to lift 100. Not much difference. These systems are supposed to be 9:1 and 6:1 respectively but a lot of force is lost through friction!

This highlights the difference between *ideal mechanical advantage* (e.g. 9:1) and *theoretical mechanical advantage:* the resulting mechanical advantage once friction generated by pulleys, carabiners, cliff edges, etc. is accounted for. Because of the amount of efficiency lost to friction it is not always worth building more involved systems unless you have high quality pulleys.

IF YOU NEED MORE!

How large a system do you want? We already said simple is better and we know friction is eating away at our efficiency (especially if we are using carabiners instead of pulleys), but what system will be enough to get the job done? Here are a few more points to consider with raising systems.

Mechanical advantage or change of direction? Mechanical advantage explains how work is spread out over time and distance. For the purposes of improvised self-rescue, "mechanical advantage" can be thought of in these simplified terms: with a mechanical advantage ratio of 3:1, for every three feet of rope pulled through the system, your patient will be raised one foot. With a 9:1, for every nine feet of rope pulled through the system your patient will be raised one foot. When building a mechanical advantage system, if the last

pulley is attached to the anchor and is *not* moving, it is not helping with the mechanical advantage. Instead, it is termed a "change of direction." This is good if you want to pull down instead of up, but not if you are concerned about friction. It is only adding more friction to the system, not any mechanical advantage. That being said, do not be afraid to add a change of direction to any of your systems, if it will help. Note the Spanish Burton: the last pulley is moving so it *is* helping with mechanical advantage.

How big do you go? In the sidebar "Pulley versus Carabiner Efficiency" we give some real-world numbers relating to input effort for different systems to raise a 100-pound load. These numbers merely look at friction at the pulley points and do not look at friction or losses throughout the rest of the system. Building a wonderful 3:1 to pull up our 200-pound buddy is not such a rosy picture when we look at all

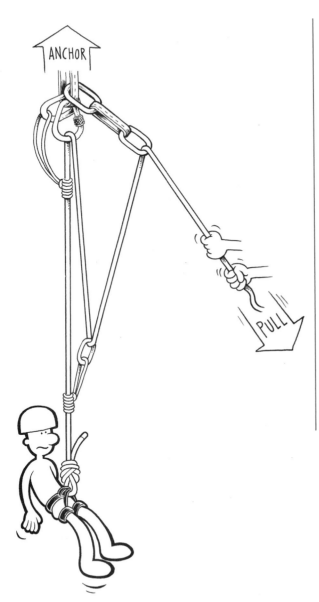

the losses in the system. If the rope runs sharply over an edge, say a 90-degree bend (ouch!), you can lose as much as 50 percent of your effort. That means if you have a 3:1 built with climbing pulleys (83 percent efficiency), and your rope runs over a bare rock edge down to the 200-pound patient, you need to pull with 120 pounds! You would only have to pull with 80 pounds if that edge was not there. (Reducing edge angles is another reason to rig high.)

One easy way to increase your system's efficiency is to replace carabiners used as pulley points with actual pulleys. Some climbers would say you are foolish to head up a long multipitch climb without a pulley. This simple substitution reduces a large amount of friction in the system. (DMM's Revolver—a carabiner with a small, built-in pulley—is a lightweight solution). If you are dealing with obstacles like sharp edges, don't forget to consider protecting your rope with some impromptu edge protection: extra clothes, a pack, an ice ax shaft, and so on. Remember to secure the item to the anchor.

Fig. 6-8. Because the quickdraw coming off the anchor is stationary it does not add mechanical advantage to this 3:1 pulley. All the quickdraw does is provide a change of direction so that the belayer can pull downwards. Because of the added friction the change of direction carbiner creates, it would make more sense to raise with a Spanish Burton (a 3:1 that already incorporates a downward pull).

Keeping the system clean, simple, and straight will get you more bang for your effort than adding advantage with pulleys to an inefficient system. But if inefficiencies are unavoidable, then yes, you may need to look at adding more mechanical advantage. Note also that the forces you are putting on your anchor when raising are much higher than in normal climbing scenarios. Do you need to beef up your anchor? If you pull on a system and there is something stuck, like a knot in a crack, and you continue pulling, the forces exerted on the anchor could skyrocket. A good rule of thumb when building these systems is that you should definitely be able to feel the load when you pull on the system; this also helps safeguard against pulling your patient up through an obstacle (a ledge, vegetation, a crevasse lip, a stuck section of rope, etc.), which could result in serious injury and putting undue forces on the anchor.

TURNING A SIMPLE 3:1 INTO A COMPLEX 5:1

This is a nice little system that allows you some more mechanical advantage: a 5:1, with just a little adjusting.

1. Clip a long single strand length of webbing or cord through your anchor's shelf. (The longer the piece of webbing the better.)

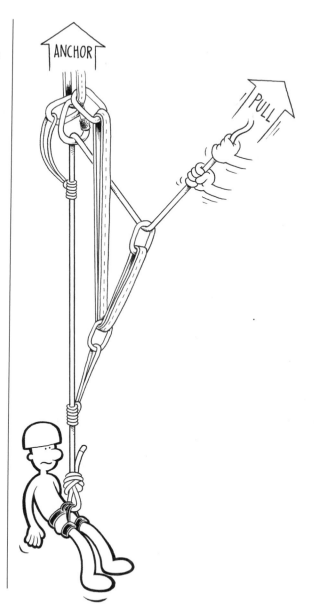

Fig. 6-9. A complex 5:1. A 3:1 can be quickly turned into a 5:1 with the addition of just two carabiners and a piece of webbing.

2. Clip the webbing through the carabiner attached to the pulley-point Prusik.
3. Clip the haul line through a carabiner attached to the other end of the webbing strand. (See fig. 6-9.)

MULTIPLYING ADVANTAGE

The basic 2:1 and 3:1 are excellent for the majority of needs; sometimes you might want a system with bigger mechanical advantage, like the 5:1 systems described above. It is also possible to gain much more advantage, without making the system too involved, by stacking systems. If you build a 2:1 to pull (act on) a 3:1, you get a 6:1—the advantage is multiplied. So if you pull on a 3:1 acting on a 3:1, you get a 9:1. That's a lot of force! Again, your anchors need to be able to handle the forces you create; and the forces are higher than ideal due to friction in the system. Friction in the system also makes the higher mechanical advantage systems much less efficient unless you include some pulleys in place of carabiners.

Generally, on a small rock ledge space is an issue, so stacking systems is tough to do. On a glacier there is more space to work, so it is easier to build bigger, more complex systems. Keep it simple. It is often more efficient to pull harder than it is to add more carabiners (friction) and bends in the rope (friction).

Raising systems can get quite involved, and we do not discuss the more complex systems that may be used in larger rescues.

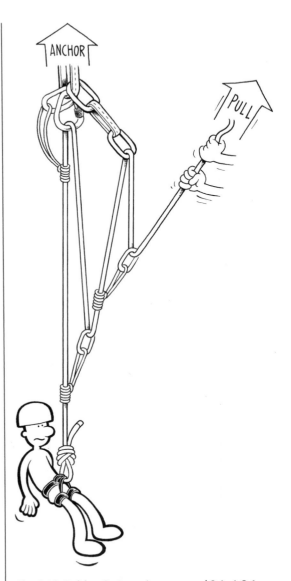

Fig. 6-10. Raising System. A compound 9:1. A 3:1 acting on a 3:1.

In reality, the 2:1 and 3:1 presented above should take care of a majority of small-party rescue situations. If you need more complex systems, you also may need more people and more gear than you have with you. Just because you can build it does not mean your equipment can handle it. Remember to tie off the original system when you are in the process of adding advantage.

BUILDING A 2:1 ACTING ON A 3:1

1. Take a long sling, cord, or the standing end of the rope. Clip it directly to the anchor.
2. Tie a Prusik with a rescue loop on the haul line of the 3:1 and clip a locking carabiner to it (this is a second, new pulley-point carabiner).
3. Clip your new piece of sling/cord/rope (introduced in step 1) through the new pulley-point carabiner.
4. Push both pulley-point carabiners down the lines as far as possible while the ratchet Prusik holds the load.
5. Haul on the new piece of sling/cord/rope.
6. You are now using a compound 6:1. Reset the pulley-point Prusiks as necessary.

BUILDING A 3:1 ACTING ON A 3:1

1. Clip a locking carabiner in to the MP or shelf of your anchor.
2. Slide the pulley-point Prusik down the rope as far as possible.
3. Tie a Prusik with a rescue loop on the haul line of the 3:1 and clip a locker to it (just as in step 2 of "Building a 2:1 Acting on a 3:1").
4. Clip the haul line through the new locker on the anchor and then run it back down and clip it through the locker on the rescue loop.
5. You now have a compound 9:1. Pull and reset the pulley-point Prusiks as necessary.

CHAPTER 7

Though it looks like a mess, passing knots is a simple process.

Passing Knots

Passing a knot can be a necessary maneuver in all sorts of situations: ascending or descending a fixed line, hauling, rappelling, or belaying—in short, any time two ropes have been tied together to create one, long continuous line or there is a knot isolating a damaged section of rope.

The common element, no matter what direction you are moving on the rope (or are moving someone else via belaying or hauling), is to maintain a secure connection to the rope at all times while moving around the knot—*around* being the key word.

ASCENDING AND DESCENDING

Regardless of whether you are using mechanical ascenders or an ascension rig, these same steps apply for passing a knot while ascending or descending. We describe both processes with the climber using a tied ascension rig.

ASCENDING

1. Ascend until your waist Prusik is within an inch or two of the knot.
2. Attach a cordelette (preferably a rescue loop) with a friction hitch above the knot. This will become your new waist Prusik.
3. Stand in your foot Prusik and, with a carabiner clipped through your belay loop, clip in to the new waist Prusik.
4. Hang on the new waist Prusik and remove the old waist Prusik (reset the old waist Prusik above the knot if you need to keep using it, that is, if the length of the new waist Prusik makes ascending inefficient).
5. Continue ascending until your foot Prusik hits the knot. Remove your foot Prusik and reset it above the knot.

You have passed the knot and can continue ascending the line.

IMPROVISE: PASSING A KNOT ON A SINGLE-STRAND LINE

If you know you will be descending or ascending a single-strand line with a knot prior to loading the line, here is a useful variation. We use rappelling as an example. This technique will not work as described with double ropes; it can only be implemented on a fixed, single-strand line.

1. When tying two ropes together, leave an extra foot of tail on the side exiting closest to the ground. Tie a figure eight on a bight (overhand on a bight if you do not have enough line) in that tail.

2. When you arrive at the knot you need to pass, simply clip in to the knot tied on the tail with some sort of tether. This becomes your primary attachment to the rope.

3. Follow steps previously described in "Ascending." Transition your weight back onto your descent device. Do not forget to take your foot Prusik with you!

The last person to use the knot tied on the tail should undo it to avoid possible snagging when the rope is either pulled up or dropped.

Fig. 7-1. Passing a knot on a single strand line. Clipping into the figure eight on a bight tied on the Flemish bend's tail provides a quick and easy way to back yourself up as you pass the knot.

DESCENDING

To descend, follow the same process as ascending, but in reverse:

1. Descend until your foot Prusik is at the knot and your waist Prusik is 4 to 5 inches above the knot. While weighting your waist Prusik, remove your foot Prusik and reset it on the line right below the knot.
2. Place a temporary waist Prusik below the knot with a friction hitch and transfer your body weight down to it.
3. Reset your main waist Prusik below the knot. Simple!

Note: Either ascending or descending, it is possible to pass the knot without a spare waist Prusik, but you will need to stand in your foot loop, remove your waist Prusik, and replace it all with one hand. For the short time during which you remove your waist Prusik, you are only attached to the rope by one means: your foot Prusik. This is a good reason for tying in short every 10 feet or so with a figure eight on a bight. If you are unable to, due to weight at the end of the line or it being fixed, be cautious and make sure you are backed up, attached to the line at two points.

RAPPELLING

In order to pass a knot while rappelling, you need your hands free to manipulate the rope; anticipate this and have some sort of backup belay in place before you start heading down. The process of passing a knot on rappel is the same regardless of if you are rappelling one strand of rope or two. (See fig. 7-2.)

1. About 6 inches to a foot before your rappel device hits the knot, stop, let your third hand engage, achieving "hands-free," and pull out your cordelette.
2. Pull up about 10 feet of the rappel line, and then tie a figure eight on a bight and clip it to your belay loop with a locking carabiner as a backup. Use both rope strands if it is a double-strand rappel.
3. Tie your long cordelette in a loop using a bend, and attach it to the rappel ropes with a Prusik hitch a few inches above your belay device.
4. Clip a locking carabiner in to your belay loop, and with the excess cordelette tail, tie a Munter-mule-overhand (MMO) onto the carabiner. (This is the PMMO sequence, just tied and attached in a different place.)
5. Push the Prusik up the line, removing as much slack as possible. (Take care to create the MMO in a tight package so that it does not get pushed up out of reach).
6. Lower yourself onto the cordelette using your rappel device.
7. With the cordelette holding your weight, remove your rappel device and reset it on the line just below the knot.
8. Reset your third hand onto the rope below your rappel device. Or tie off the rappel with leg wraps or a mule-overhand.

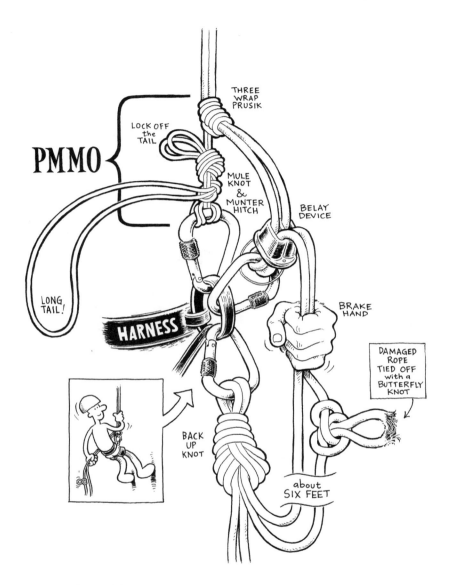

Fig. 7-2. Passing a knot while rappelling. The PMMO tied with the cordalette will hold the climber's weight as he moves his belay device around the damaged section of rope. He can then employ the Munter to transfer his weight back onto his belay device. Once the weight transfer is complete he will remove the cordalette from the climbing rope. The figure eight on a bight serves as a backup while he passes the knot.

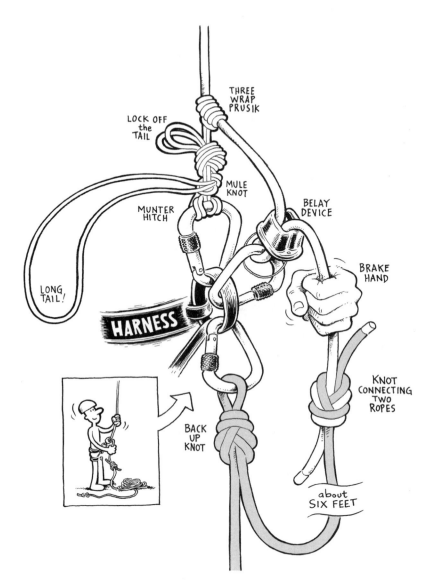

THREE WRAP PRUSIK

LOCK OFF the TAIL

MULE KNOT

MUNTER HITCH

BELAY DEVICE

BRAKE HAND

LONG TAIL!

HARNESS

KNOT CONNECTING TWO ROPES

BACK UP KNOT

about SIX FEET

Fig. 7-3. Passing a knot while top-rope lowering. If a second belayer is not available to help you with passing a knot while top-rope belaying you will need to tie a PMMO with a cordalette. The process is almost identical to passing a knot on rappel; the cordalette holds the climber's weight while you move the belay device around the knot, then use the cordalette to transfer the weight back onto the belay device.

SETTING THE PRUSIK CORRECTLY

The length of the loop you create on your cordelette and where you tie the Prusik that attaches your cordelette to the rope are both important. If you do not get these measures right, you will end up wasting a lot of time, hanging in an uncomfortable position. For example, take a look at passing a knot on rappel. If you tie your Prusik on too high up, you will never be able to reach it once you move around the knot. But if you do not make your cordelette loop long enough, you will have a tough time getting back onto your belay device. In that same vein, if you rappel down too close to the knot, you will have trouble getting out of your rappel device. All these reasons make passing a knot on rappel a good skill to practice.

9. Undo the mule overhand tied with the cordelette on your carabiner and slowly lower yourself back onto the climbing rope using the cordelette's Munter hitch.
10. Once you have transferred your weight back onto your rappel device, you can unthread the Munter, and reach up and remove the Prusik hitch from the top line.
11. Undo your backup tie-in and start rappelling again.

ON A TOP ROPE

TOP-ROPE BELAYING

The simplest way to pass a knot while top-rope belaying is to employ the help of another person:

1. Belay the climber as normal until you are just 1 to 2 inches from the knot. At this point, ask the climber to wait for a moment on the climb.
2. Take a couple steps forward and have the third person clip her belay device in to the climber strand on the other side of the knot.
3. The belay is immediately transferred to your recruited helper.
4. The new belayer can start taking in slack as the climber climbs. You can unclip your belay device from your harness if you want, or leave it on for the lowering transition (described below).

If you do not have another person at your disposal, start at a new step 2:

2. With a little slack in the climbing line, load a second belay device onto the rope above the knot. (Assuming the climber can temporarily unweight the rope, you may want to do some leg wraps with the belay line to free your hands for this.)
3. Attach this second belay device to your harness and start belaying. You can leave the first one on for the lowering transition.

TOP-ROPE LOWERING

The simplest way to pass a knot while top-rope lowering is, again, to employ the help of another person:

1. As described above, you transferred the climber to your recruited helper's belay device; now the helper starts the lower once the climb is finished. Have your helper lower the climber all the way to the knot.

2. At this point, let your climber know you need to pass the knot. If possible have him unweight the rope by using a good foothold, handhold, or ledge. If he is unable to do this, things will be a bit harder for you.

3. While your helper locks off the climber's belay (the knot is a great backup here), put your belay device on below the knot. If you passed this knot while the climber was going up, you may have left your device attached to the rope, and all you need to do is reattach the device to your harness.

4. Let your partner know you are ready to continue belaying.

5. Have your helper step forward and unclip her belay device from her harness. It can remain on the line while you finish lowering the climber.

For both passing a knot while top-rope belaying or lowering, the steps are the same if you are by yourself. It is best to get hands-free to do the transitions from one belay device to another.

See fig. 7-3 for instructions as to how to pass a knot while top roping. The steps are very similar to passing a knot on rappel as previously described.

LOWERING ON THE ANCHOR

1. About 10 inches before the knot ("1A" in fig. 7-4) reaches the Munter hitch, free your hands with a mule. Rather than tying an overhand back-up clip the mule's loop off with a carabiner; it saves rope and keeps the system short. (See the completed mule and backup "1B" in fig. 7-5).

2. Tie a friction hitch (a Prusik) on the load strand using the cordelette (2 in fig. 7-6).

3. Tie the other end of the cordelette to a free locking carabiner (on the MP) with a MMO; this completes the PMMO (3 in fig. 7-6).

4. Take the rope beyond the offending knot and set up an MMO with this section of rope onto another locker clipped in to the anchor (4 in fig. 7-6). (Alternately, you could use a self-blocking or locking assist belay device if you had one. Insert the belay device onto the rope with a locking carabiner and tie it off with a mule overhand.) You should now have three tied-off belays in a row.

5. Undo the mule backup clip and let the Prusik hold the load (fig. 7-7).

6. Undo the MMO on the cordelette and lower the climber until the tied-off rope is loaded after the knot (fig. 7-8).

7. Undo the Prusik hitch and Munter hitch tied with the cordelette and remove the cordelette from the system (fig. 7-8).

8. Undo the mule-overhand in the rope and continue lowering the climber

PASSING A KNOT WHILE LOWERING

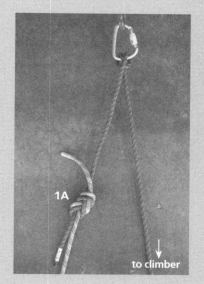

Fig. 7-4. About 10 inches before the knot (1A) reaches your belay device, prepare to free your hands with a mule hitch and backup.

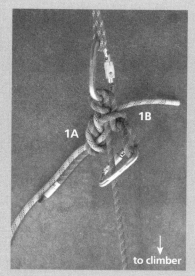

Fig. 7-5. Step 1, completed. "1A" indicates the knot to be passed; "1B" is the Munter mule and backup.

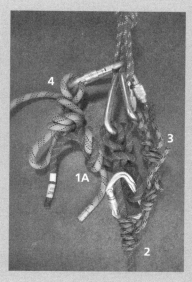

Fig. 7-6. Steps 2, 3 and 4.

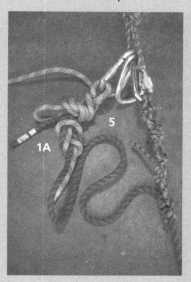

Fig. 7-7. Step 5.

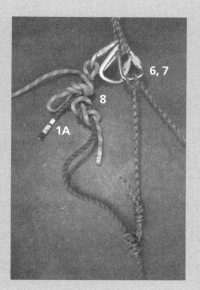

Fig. 7-8. Step 6. Once the knot is passed, remove the cordalette from the system (step 7) and undo the mule-overhand (step 8).

Fig. 7-9. Completed knot pass. Continue lowering on the Munter hitch.

PRACTICE: PASSING KNOTS

One advantage to the process of passing a knot—either while ascending, descending, or while on rappel—is that you are always attached to the rope in at least two places: by one of your Prusik knots and by the backup knots tied every 10 feet and attached to your harness. Although these backups are relatively foolproof, we still recommend practicing on the ground before going vertical and using a fixed line for backup the first time off the ground. Note: It helps when practicing to have weight on the line.

using the Munter now that the knot has been passed.

RAISING

If you are unfamiliar with the construction and anatomy of raising systems, you will find it useful to read chapter 6, Raising, in order to gain an understanding of what this technique is all about.

These steps are for use on a 3:1 raising system. Other systems will be similarly easy. The knot will first appear below the moving pulley-point Prusik on the load strand.

1. When resetting the pulley-point Prusik, simply loosen and move the Prusik hitch to the climber side of the knot.

2. Continue hauling until the knot is just a few inches away from the ratchet Prusik.

3. While the ratchet does its job—holding the weight of the climber without letting him slip back down—make a new ratchet on the other side of the knot. You can construct this extra

ratchet many ways: use a short rescue loop to tie a Prusik and then clip the rescue loop to the anchor with a sling (you can also just use a long cordelette). It is easier to pass the knot if the new ratchet is longer than the original one.

4. Haul a bit more to transfer the load to the new ratchet—you will have to set the new ratchet (to allow it to hold your patient's weight) and then remove the old ratchet.

5. Clip a new locking carabiner to the MP. Tie a backup knot on the free end of the haul line and clip it into the locking carabiner. (This is the system backup.)

6. Haul your partner a few more inches until the knot is against the anchor pulley point or your belay device. Make sure the ratchet is engaged, and then move the MP around the knot onto the new line. You may need to extend the MP with a runner to get the knot to the other side. Once the knot is passed, undo the backup knot and continue hauling.

ISOLATING ROPE DAMAGE

A butterfly is the knot of choice for isolating rope damage.

1. Take a bight of rope and turn it in a full circle. The rope will cross itself over in two sections creating a top loop, a middle loop, and a "bight"(for lack of a better term) on the bottom.

2. Take the top loop and bring it down and under the "bight" through to the other side. (Make it easier on yourself by bringing the loop in whichever direction maintains the structure of the top loop.)

3. Continue, bringing the top loop through the middle loop. (You will actually be traveling through two loops, the second one resulting from the top loop having folded downward.)

4. Pull the loop through until snug and dress.

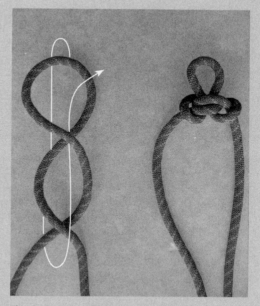

Fig. 7-10. Butterfly knot. Left: Step 1, with arrow indicating steps 2 and 3. Right: Completed knot

CHAPTER 8

Big mountains, high altitude, and technical terrain are a recipe for the unexpected.

Scenarios and Solutions

Here is an opportunity to test your knowledge and understanding of the techniques covered in this book and to hone your problem-solving capabilities by looking at incidents that really have happened in the vertical world.

Each scenario presented is followed by a solution, a discussion of potential pitfalls (if any), tips for prevention, and a list of skills to review (not all skills to review are discussed in this book; we highlight those necessary to solve the situation). In addition to the primary solution, viable alternatives may be presented; generally, the solution presented first is a simple or fast option. Some scenarios have multiple solutions, but in the interest of space we have not covered all possibilities.

You will get the most benefit by working through the scenarios before reading the solutions. Formulate your own solution first. Then test yourself further by asking:

What are alternative solutions? Potential pitfalls? Ways of preventing the problem in the first place?

To test yourself even further, review the six emergency procedures discussed in chapter 1: plan ahead and prepare, assess the scene, initiate first aid, make a plan, rescue, and follow through. Imagine what these steps would look like in some of the areas where you enjoy climbing.

Note: Scenarios range from the simple to the complex. Invariably you may disagree with us on our approach to a particular scenario or solution. But regardless of if you breeze through a scenario or find yourself scratching your head, the exercise will be helping you to meet the goal of developing critical-thinking climbing skills.

We assume that you have the following equipment with you:
- One single dynamic rope per party, 50–60 meters (160–200 ft)

- Second rope indicated if a part of the scenario
- Six nonlocking carabiners
- Either a traditional or sport climbing rack for the leader
- Six locking carabiners
- Forty feet of 7-millimeter accessory cord
- cut into five lengths (discussed in text)
- Some webbing for creating runners
- Tubular belay device (like an ATC)
- UIAA-rated harness
- UIAA-rated helmet
- A small knife

SCENARIO 1

You have been struggling on the third and final pitch of this traditional route for quite a while; in fact, you are so tired from the previous attempts, you have given up. You yell up to your belayer that you need a boost, but no luck. She does not seem to hear you. Your belayer mainly sport climbs and you are pretty sure she is not familiar with raising systems or assists. What can you do to get yourself past the crux besides praying for a sudden miracle?

SOLUTION

It's a trad route so you should have cleaned a bit of gear from the route that could be placed and used as a point of aid. Considering the gear's application (you are on belay from above) it doesn't need to be a bomber piece of gear; just make sure it's attached to something in case it blows. You hopefully also have some slings and cordelettes with which to quickly make an ascension rig if you can't French-free your way up.

POTENTIAL PITFALLS

If you end up ascending, be careful when you start climbing on the rock again, after you have Prusiked past the crux. Slowly slide your Prusiks off the rope so that your partner can take up the slack with the belay. Do not just climb with your Prusiks on the line and a loop of slack below you.

PREVENTION

Pick appropriate routes. Do not wear yourself out on one particular move. Always be prepared—in particular, know what your partner is capable of and what you might have to do for yourself.

SKILLS TO REVIEW

French-freeing, tying an ascension rig and ascending a fixed line (chapter 5).

SCENARIO 2

After flying into Denver International Airport from Florida, you and your partner rent a car and head straight for Rocky Mountain National Park. Less than 24 hours later, you are standing on the summit of a pinnacle (elevation: close to 13,000 feet). Throughout the several-hour, seven-pitch climb, your partner has not been feeling quite himself (he chalks it up to being dehydrated). He continues to deteriorate and at the summit he tells you he feels like he is on the verge of passing out; he is nervous about his ability to rappel. How will the two of you safely descend? There is no walk-off.

SOLUTIONS

There are multiple solutions to this scenario, the simplest being to tandem rappel as long as you trust your anchors with your and your partner's combined weight. This way you would be with your partner if he faints.

You could also employ a cow's tail for your partner's rappel rig. Back him up with a fireman's belay as he makes his way down. Remember, as the first rappeller, to use a third hand as a backup.

PREVENTION

Rapid changes in altitude, as experienced in this scenario, can take their toll on the body in many ways, especially if compounded by dehydration, exhaustion, or a calorie deficit. Give yourself time to acclimatize. Perhaps your partner should have spoken up about his condition earlier.

SKILLS TO REVIEW

Tandem rappelling, third-hand backup, fireman's belay (chapter 4)

SCENARIO 3

While traveling on a popular glacier route, your partner falls into a crevasse. You are traveling in a team of two. You quickly set up a compound 9:1 raising system. Your partner has fallen 30 feet and the process is slowgoing. Soon another two-person team arrives on the scene. How can you best use these additional people to help you?

SOLUTION

Drop that raising system down. The higher a raising system's mechanical advantage, the less the distance you are actually raising your patient per pull. Turn it back to a 3:1 and haul on it. It will be faster and easier for everyone.

POTENTIAL PITFALLS

Pulling on a big-advantage system with a lot of people can be hard on your anchors, gear, and patient. Remember while pulling that you should still feel your patient's weight to guard against injuring him.

PREVENTION

Crevasse falls are part of the risk of traveling through glaciated terrain. There are of course several measures that can be taken to improve your chances of safe travel: using a probe, receiving a more formal belay, and/or crawling on all fours over suspicious snow bridges. If you find yourself punching through consistently, it is important to consider if it is really appropriate to be traveling in crevasse country in such conditions. Should you be traveling instead at night, when it is cooler, or wait a day to see if conditions firm up?

SKILLS TO REVIEW

3:1 and 9:1 raising systems (see chapter 6)

SCENARIO 4

Your climbing partner is following your trad lead, struggling desperately with a route's crux move. After 15 minutes, he gives up. Spent, he asks you for assistance. He is about 15 meters from the belay station. What is the simplest way for you to assist him and/or for him to help himself?

SOLUTIONS

There are a variety of solutions to this scenario, ranging from simple to overkill and complicated. First: Your partner can always pull on the runners of the gear placed above him for assistance (in lead climbing this is called "using a point of aid" or French-freeing). If he has any extra runners, gathered from cleaning the rest of the route, he can girth-hitch several together to create a makeshift etrier to help him through the crux. He can also place any gear he has with him, accumulated from cleaning the route, into the crack and employ the techniques listed above.

If none of the above solutions work, the next easiest thing is to get your hands free with a mule-overhand. Then secure a section of the brake strand to the anchor with a figure eight on a bight or a clove hitch, and lower the remaining slack down to him. Because it is a fixed line, he can pull on it all he wants for assistance while you continue belaying him up. If for some reason he cannot pull, the next option would be a drop-line assist.

POTENTIAL PITFALLS

If your partner had not yet climbed close enough to the belay, then you would not have enough rope to send down to him. You would have to rely on a more involved raising system such as a 3:1.

PREVENTION

It is worth asking yourself as the leader if this route is appropriate for your partner. Had you anticipated that your partner might have problems, you could have set a piece with a long sling (or created an etrier by girth-hitching several slings/runners together to the desired length) above the crux—long enough so that he could reach it and pull himself up through the crux. Consider if you should do something similar for the following pitches.

SKILLS TO REVIEW

Mule-overhand (chapter 2), getting hands-free (chapter 3), French-freeing (chapter 5), drop line assist (chapter 6)

SCENARIO 5

You are belaying your friend at a popular top-rope site with a lot of other climbers around. He pulls off a large rock that falls and significantly damages the rope 3 feet below your brake hand on the belay strand. Your partner is shaken and wants to be lowered. How will you get him down? *Note:* You can borrow a second climbing rope from a nearby climber if desired.

SOLUTION

Tie your partner off with a mule-overhand to free your hands. Then isolate the damaged section of rope with a butterfly knot. Ask a nearby climber, Rita, to come over and put your partner on belay after the knot. Untie the mule-overhand and lower your partner until you hit the knot. Make sure that Rita has the belay and then unclip your device from your harness. Rita continues lowering your partner to the ground (your carabiner and belay device can stay on the rope).

If the rope is completely severed, then borrow a second rope from a nearby climber and tie the two ropes together using a double fisherman's or Flemish bend. You will still need to pass the knot.

POTENTIAL PITFALLS

What if you are alone at the base? Free your hands, tie a butterfly or retie the two severed strands together, put a second locker into your harness, and tie a Munter-mule-overhand (MMO) onto that carabiner after the knot. You then can lower your partner and when you reach the knot, ask him to unweight the rope by holding onto a feature on the climb. Take the necessary steps for passing a knot on a top-rope lower.

PREVENTION

Watch where you belay for a top rope. Generally you have options for this type of setup. If you know the route has loose rock, site the belay out of firing range.

SKILLS TO REVIEW

MMO (chapter 2), passing a knot while lowering, and butterfly (chapter 7)

SCENARIO 6

You hear cries for help coming from a ledge far below that you are about to rappel over after a day of cragging. You are able to talk with the person shouting. The climber says that he has been trying to practice an aid-climbing technique that he read about. His last piece pulled out and he smashed his hand and can't get out of the system. You are able to see that he is dangling from the end of a rope that is girth-hitched to a locking carabiner on his harness. He is 50 feet off the ground and 5 feet below his last piece. How will you help him?

SOLUTION

Continue setting up your rappel, but rig your rappel device for a tandem rappel with either two cow's tails or a rescue spider. Rappel to just above the climber. Free your hands by using a third-hand backup and assist him by helping him clip the cow's tail (or rescue spider) to his harness. The injured climber needs to unweight his locking carabiner at this point. Have him pull up on your rope while you undo his attachment, or set up a short sling for him (to pull on or step into) attached to your rope with a Prusik hitch. Once he is separated from his system continue as a tandem rappel to the ground. Deal with his gear separately.

POTENTIAL PITFALLS

Avoid rappelling below the injured climber. That will make the transfer more difficult. Don't worry about his stuff. Just get him safely to the ground. He messed up one system already; don't let him mess up yours too. You are the rescuer, so take charge and make sure he does what you want him to do.

PREVENTION

His aid system was flawed; he used a girth hitch rather than a clove. He should have had Prusik slings along to get himself out of his jam.

SKILLS TO REVIEW

Rappelling on a cow's tail, tandem rappelling, weight transfer, pick-off (chapter 4)

SCENARIO 7

You and your partner have just completed a linkup of two long ice routes. It is now well after dark and you are in the middle of rappelling off the top of the second 500-foot ice route. You are using two ropes to rappel. Your partner raps and shortly you are both down at the next V-thread, optimistic that you will be back at the car in an hour. You carefully pull the rope, watching as one end pulls out of view, making sure that there are no knots, and the rope starts whipping down as expected. But it stops. "No big deal," you think. "It must have gotten hung up somewhere." On ice routes this often can be easily fixed by just pulling harder. But the rope does not budge. The temperature is -30°C; you are tired, cold, and really just want to get back to the warmth of the truck. What to do? Rappelling down the next 300 feet of ice would be a real pain with only one rope, plus if you leave a rope you are looking at a round trip of 10+ hours the following day to retrieve it; by then it may well be covered in new ice and impossible to get.

What are your options for getting off the route? After short debate over the efficiency (and expense) of continuing on just one rope versus releading the pitch to retrieve the stuck one, you opt for the latter. Although it is cold and dark, as a team you feel comfortable with the situation. (If it were an emergency you would not hesitate to leave gear.) How will you go about retrieving the stuck rope? How could it have gotten stuck in the first place?

SOLUTION

First, beef up the V-thread so that it is now adequate as a lead-climbing anchor, not just a rappel anchor. Put a waist Prusik on the stuck rope and clip it to your harness as a backup; your partner puts you back on belay with the second rope. You lead back up the route, placing screws regularly. At the top you realize why the rope stuck; there is a perfect overhand knot 2 feet from the end of the rope. You are positive that knot was not there when you started rappelling—you pulled the rope and double-checked. Somehow while being pulled the rope whipped around in the air creating a knot. Although a rare occurrence, this definitely can and does happen. Continue on to the anchor, reset the rope for a rappel, and hurry back down.

POTENTIAL PITFALLS

Considering that it is the end of a long day, make sure you as a leader are up for the lead and that your partner will be warm enough for belaying.

PREVENTION

Knots happen; rappel ropes get stuck; be ready for it.

SKILLS TO REVIEW

Dealing with stuck ropes (chapter 4). Ascending a fixed line (chapter 5)

SCENARIO 8

While cleaning the pitch you just led, your partner falls. Due to the loud roar of the stream below, you are unable to speak with him to determine his condition. Several minutes have passed and there is still no movement on his end of the rope. You decide to escape the belay so you can more accurately assess the scene and determine what sort of assistance he needs. It is a hanging belay and you are belaying off your body. However, because you clipped in to the longest link on your daisy chain so you could reach a comfortable belay stance, you can't reach the anchor—it is just out of arm's reach. How will you escape the belay?

SOLUTION

If you are on a daisy, the anchor can't be that far out of reach. Get hands-free from the belay. Lean into the rock and stretch as far as possible to get a carabiner onto the anchor. If you *really* can't reach it, escape the belay and move it onto your daisy (although this is by *no* means ideal) as close to the anchor as you can put the system. Once you can move up a bit, transfer the weight again off your daisy and on to the MP as soon as possible.

POTENTIAL PITFALLS

Daisy chains are not meant for this type of application. They are for clipping in to a system, but many are only rated for body weight. They are not intended to hold you and your belay. It is surprisingly easy to blow the sewn pockets on several brands of daisy chains with dynamic loading. When you move the belay to the daisy, watch out that your climber is not getting ready to try the route again, potentially generating a fall load right onto the daisy. Check the manufacturer's instructions for the proper application of your daisy.

PREVENTION

Using the climbing rope as an anchor tether has many advantages as illustrated by this scenario. This way you will always have a fixed section of rope available for rescue purposes (assisting or raising your partner), and can easily extend the anchor. If you've chosen to use a tether instead and the climbing rope is not connected to the anchor in any way, make sure to stay within an arm's reach of the anchor or take the steps to extend your anchor ahead of time. We do not recommend using daisy chains for extending anchors.

SKILLS TO REVIEW

Escaping a belay (chapter 3)

Note: Scenarios 9–12 include multiple characters.

SCENARIO 9

Kelly is part of a group of three on a five-pitch climb in Wyoming. The group is trying to move faster with an advanced technique: The leader leads the pitch on one rope while dragging a second one. At the belay he puts both his partners on belay and they climb together while he belays them at the same time, with a self-blocking belay device like a GiGi (Reverso, B-52, etc.).

Pat leads the third pitch, trailing two ropes, and then puts Kelly and Chris on belay. Kelly climbs first, and then Chris starts out after Kelly about 10 feet above him. The pitch is challenging for both of them. About halfway up Chris is tired and having trouble with the climb. He falls and swings 10 feet off the line of the climb. It is even harder where he is and he can't climb any farther.

Pat forgot to take the GiGi from the last leader when he started leading and so he used his ATC as a belay device instead. He put one climber's rope through one hole and one through the second hole and has been belaying both climbers by pulling in the lines, using his fingers to separate them and pull up slack whenever he feels one of them move. He is on a nice ledge, with the anchor situated down low at the back, so he is sitting, tied in to the anchor with a clove hitch and belaying directly off his harness.

It is windy so communication is hard. The team discussed communicating in the wind (with rope tugs for on and off belay), talked about who and which color rope would climb first, but did not solidify a plan. None of them has used this technique of double seconding before. Kelly and Chris are not able to communicate what the situation is to Pat. Kelly, still able to climb but getting tired, has tried to continue climbing, but Pat is not taking up the rope slack. Pat has locked his ATC to hold Chris, so he is unable to take in Kelly's rope. What can Kelly do? What can Chris and Pat do?

SOLUTIONS

For Kelly: Kelly does not have many options. He is in Pat's hands. He can coach Chris on the moves and encourage him higher, but his independent progress is limited by the locked ATC (of which he is unaware). He can try and communicate with Pat by directing his voice toward the belay and yelling clear simple statements, but only the conditions will tell if that is effective.

If he is on terrain that is easy, he can try climbing up, creating a bit of slack in his rope and then tying in short with a knot clipped to a locking carabiner on his belay loop. If the terrain is too difficult, he can use a friction hitch to ascend the line or use friction hitches as a backup while he climbs. This would get him to the belay to help Pat. The problem with this independent progress is that Pat may not be expecting it and if Kelly falls there will be a big shock load on Pat and his belay. This is a situation for Pat to deal with. If communication becomes possible Kelly might consider climbing to the nearest piece of protection (if it is not too far) and then evaluate the piece and clip in to it if it is good. At this point, Pat could easily only lower Chris through the device.

For Pat: Though bleak at first look, there are a variety of possible solutions to this one. With time, Kelly will become tired and unable to hang on. He will eventually hang on the rope as well, at which point Pat, desperately needing a solution, will probably decide to just lower his partners. Hopefully Chris will be able to swing over to the last belay anchor. Kelly may need to provide a helpful pull.

Another option for Pat is to quickly tie off Chris (maybe with some leg wraps) and extend the anchor (with the tail of his tie-in as described in Scenerio 8). Then, if there is enough slack in Kelly's line, he can tie a MMO with Kelly's rope onto the extended anchor. The MMO can function as a lock-off on Kelly's position while Pat lowers Chris, or Pat can fully escape both belays, transferring both to the anchor. Pat can make a longer tether for himself to get farther from the anchor (he will probably need a sling to do that and then untie from his tie-in knot). Now Pat may be able to see what is going on down there and maybe communicate better. At this point—with the belay now on the anchor—the two climbers' belays are separated. Each climber is free to move up and Chris can be lowered if need be. They have to be independently belayed at this point.

POTENTIAL PITFALLS

If Pat tries to mess with the ATC to get it to release, he may be able to lower Chris but he will lose his belay on Kelly. Perhaps the biggest risk is if the climbers begin trying to rescue themselves all at the same time, working independently of one another. Communication is imperative!

PREVENTION

This is a good scenario for prevention. Painfully obvious is the fact that this whole situation could have been prevented by taking the GiGi in the first place. Another obvious prevention tip is to be familiar with techniques before using them—Pat should not have just used his ATC. He should have resorted to individually belaying his partners. Even with difficult communication, he would not have had to relay that. He could have just started belaying the climber he was supposed to start with, not taking in slack on the second climber until the first was at the belay with him.

SKILLS TO REVIEW

Escaping the belay (chapter 3), fixed line ascensions (chapter 5)

SCENARIO 10

You and Pat are swapping leads on a multipitch climb in front of another party. You are leading a pitch that is challenging for you. You place good protection, but add runners that are too short. Your rope zigzags back and forth, creating a lot of rope drag. High on the pitch and out of sight of your belayer (Pat), you can't pull the rope up any more due to the drag. You are runout about 20 feet above your last piece and are not able to downclimb. You yell down to Pat, "I'm stuck, I can't go up and I can't go down!" The other party reaches the anchor just as you begin shouting to Pat. How could they help you? How would your options change if Pat had a second rope?

SOLUTIONS

In this case, there is another party climbing up the route. They might be able to climb up the pitch a bit and unclip some of the offending drag pieces. This might allow you to finish the route safely. It would not be good to have the other party do this if it puts Pat or you in danger, if the other party is inexperienced, or if they might fall into your system.

Although undesirable, it might be best to attempt downclimbing. Pat can give a very attentive belay while you carefully reverse your route. If you fall, Pat is ready to catch.

A much more involved option is for Pat to escape the belay. If Pat feels comfortable with the climb's grade (or even with just the initial part of the pitch) and has a second rope, he could rope-solo up the route, either extending the runners on the already placed pieces of gear or replacing the protection in a straighter line. It may be that changes made to just the first section of the pitch will be enough to allow you to continue up or to downclimb to extend some of your pieces. Before you proceed though, Pat needs to descend back to the bottom anchor and put you back on belay.

POTENTIAL PITFALLS

A big leader fall is possible with large forces on top pieces—watch out. The leader should remain in control of the situation and direct the action before the belayer starts running around trying to fix the situation.

PREVENTION

Placing gear and adding runners so that the rope runs smoothly in a line up the route reduces the forces on individual pieces in the event of a fall, as well as avoiding the dreaded rope drag. Rope drag naturally occurs just as a result of the rope running over and around corners of rock, so adding climber-induced rope drag with poor runner lengths in addition is a recipe for challenge. Also, watch those runouts!

SKILLS TO REVIEW

Escaping a belay (chapter 3), rope soloing (chapter 5)

SCENARIO 11

This scenario uses the characters Pat and Chris described in scenario 9.

Pat starts up from the hanging belay at the top of the second pitch on a five-pitch route in Arizona. It is not possible to get in any gear for the first 30 feet of the pitch, but after the first move the climbing is easy. The route goes up about 10 feet then traverses over about 20 feet to the right, where there are large chicken heads (big plates of solid granite) heading up and angling slightly left for the rest of the climb. Since he has no protection so far and is looking at a swinging 40-plus-foot factor 2 fall onto the anchor, Pat places a sling on the nearest chicken head before the climb angles back left. He climbs the rest of the pitch, finding excellent, regular protection, and sets another hanging chicken head belay after climbing a full rope-length. Pat sets up a Munter belay off the anchor and calls "on belay" to his partner, Chris.

Chris takes out the anchor and starts to climb. He underestimates the first move and falls. Unfortunately, because of where the first piece is, he swings violently down and pendulums to the right about 20 feet and is left hanging 30 feet below the first piece of protection. The wall where he is now is blank and overhanging. There is not an anchor in sight below him for more than a rope length. What to do? What if it is windy and they can't see each other so they can't communicate?

SOLUTION

Pat: Pat does not have much rope, since Chris fell right off the anchor, so Pat can't really lower him anywhere. Pat does not have much rope to raise him either; it also would not make sense to just start raising your second if he fell, particularly if you cannot communicate with him. Try to assess the injury first. Because communication is poor, Pat is worried that Chris could be hurt. Pat needs to move to a place where he can communicate with Chris. He ties off the belay and descends the line using an ascension rig in order to communicate. He will then need to Prusik back up and set up a raising system if Chris is unable to ascend on his own.

Chris: If there is no communication, since Chris is hanging in space, the only thing he could really do is take out his waist and foot Prusiks and start climbing the line (a fixed-rope ascent). If Pat did not evaluate the traversing fall, he may not realize that Chris is hanging in space. Hopefully they can communicate.

POTENTIAL PITFALLS

Difficulty in communication is the key here; it's important that Pat realizes that Chris is in trouble. If Pat chooses to get out of the system and descend to communicate he will need to be diligent about maintaining a backup: he will need at least two Prusiks on the line attached to his harnesses. A fully extended and weighted line is a tough situation.

PREVENTION

Pat should have assessed the traversing fall hazard for his second. One easy solution would be to move the first piece of gear higher on the route. Pat could have placed his first piece to protect himself, then have moved up and placed another piece or two. He could then have downclimbed to remove his first piece. Moving the first piece higher on the route would reduce the severity of his second's swing. Also, the route above angles back to the left, so if Pat moved his first piece high enough there would be less than 20 feet to swing and his second would not drop lower than the route. This lead technique employs the same sling craft principles as described in scenario 10 (extending runners on a wandering pitch). Backcleaning should be done only with a few good pieces of protection above; leapfrogging only two pieces is not recommended, given the severity of the fall if one piece fails while leap-frogging the other.

SKILLS TO REVIEW

MMO (chapter 2), ascending a fixed line (chapter 5), raising systems (chapter 6)

It is instructive to think through your own scenarios: what would I do if she fell?

SCENARIO 12

This scenario uses the characters Pat and Chris, introduced in scenario 9.

Pat tops out and sits down in an excellent position belay (a hip belay) after an easy final pitch high on an alpine route. Chris starts climbing up. About one-third of the way up, Chris wanders off-route a bit into less climbed, steeper, and looser terrain. The rope above him catches under a rock and it dislodges, taking a nice chunk out of Chris's leg as it flies by. The impact from the rock caused Chris to fully weight the rope and he is bleeding and disoriented.

Pat is giving a hip belay with no anchor; because the route he climbed was easy and on solid rock, and thinking Chris would have no problem, Pat opted for a fast-position hip belay. After Pat yells to communicate with Chris, he realizes that Chris is dazed and might need help stopping the bleeding. Pat does a few leg wraps to free his hands, builds an anchor, and escapes the belay.

They have two ropes, but Chris is dragging the second one. Pat puts two waist Prusiks on the rope to Chris, unties from the anchor, and starts downclimbing, sliding his Prusiks down the line as a backup and removing protection as he goes. About 20 feet above Chris, the rope runs over an edge in the rock. With Chris's weight on the rope, Pat is not able to slide his Prusiks down any more, and the route is overhanging below him. He can talk to Chris, who is starting to panic due to his profusely bleeding leg. What next?

SOLUTION

Chris must find a way to get some weight off the rope. Some coaching by Pat should accomplish this. Just a foot on a good foothold and a hand on a decent handhold should allow enough slack for Pat to move his Prusiks down the line. If Chris still cannot unweight the rope, Pat will need to treat the edge like a knot and pass it. He will have to go into vertical terrain, so hopefully he brought some gear and slings to make a foot loop to comfortably descend. Once he is next to Chris, he can help with the wound and hopefully calm him down. Pat will then need to reascend the line and continue accordingly: either raise Chris or counterbalance and then tandem rappel.

POTENTIAL PITFALLS

Not having a site or gear to build an anchor. The choice to do a position belay should be based on there being a good spot to build an anchor within easy reach, should you need one. If there is not an anchor site in reach, it is not a good place to belay. Pat must also be careful to maintain his position so that he does not jeopardize his hip belay while building an anchor.

Alpine climbing requires good route finding skills.

PREVENTION

This is a tough one to prevent. The decisions along the way are appropriate. It is unfortunate that Chris wandered off-route. Pat was able to solve the no-anchor problem quickly and easily because he chose to belay in a spot with a good place to build an anchor.

SKILLS TO REVIEW

Tandem rappel and counterbalance (chapter 4), descending a fixed line (chapter 5), raising systems (chapter 6), passing a knot (chapter 7)

SCENARIO 13

While climbing a 5.7 alpine ridge traverse, bad weather moves in. You and your partner are pushing your leading ability levels and the rapidly falling fresh snow does not help either's climbing confidence. Because several of the slabs you traversed are now wet with snow and the route is notoriously runout, you do not feel comfortable backtracking or continuing. Your partner thinks you should wait the storm out in a small sheltered nook, while you—afraid that with the strong winds and cold temperatures hypothermia might set in—want to try to descend via a system of dihedrals below. After much discussion of the pros and cons of both ideas, you begin descending the dihedral system on anchors you set and then leave as you descend further.

While pulling the ropes after the second rappel, the end of the second rope gets stuck. Reluctant to lead the pitch (it is a very runout slab and the granite is now soaking wet), your partner decides to cut the rope with the small knife he carries on his harness.

You and your partner continue rappelling, having to stop and set anchors much more frequently because now you have just one 60-meter rope, your other rope being just 40 meters because you cut it. You must also pass the knot on each rappel. The process is harrowing—swinging across the wall looking for spots that will support enough gear for an anchor. At the fifth rappel station, you see nothing but blank granite below; there is no obvious crack system for building another rappel station. The ground looks approximately 90 to 110 meters away. What next?

SOLUTION

Since your ropes will not reach the ground if tied in a double-strand rappel, create a long single-strand rappel by fixing just one end of the line into the anchor, then rappel the long single strand. Approximately forty

Fast and light should not mean unprepared.

meters down, you will need to pause to pass the knot connecting the two lines together. The rope just reaches the ground.

Your partner rappels the same line, but considering that the rope is tied into the anchor (and must remain that way so that the rope reaches the ground), the ropes will have to be left behind.

POTENTIAL PITFALLS

If the rope does not reach the ground, you and your partner would plain and simple be up a creek. Using an ascension rig, you would have to ascend the rappel line (passing the knot once again) to return to the anchor.

PREVENTION

Rappelling down an unknown face, unless you carry aid gear (and potentially a hand drill and bolts), is a dicey proposition. Once the lines are pulled, you are stuck on that section of rock; there may be no easy way to ascend back up.

Do your homework and investigate your descent. Look into all options in case you have to bail early. There is no guarantee that a crack system will run the entire length of a wall, and if it does it may very well be a route noted in a guidebook.

Finally, consider getting the rope unstuck before cutting it. Often accidents happen as a result of a number of poor choices rather than one big obvious one.

SKILLS TO REVIEW

Rappelling with a backup (chapter 4), ascending (chapter 5), passing a knot (chapter 7)

SCENARIO 14

In the middle of a runout slab section, you feel your rope go taut. "SLACK!!" you yell to your friends, novice climbers, belaying below. "The rope is stuck!" they call back. Not only is the rope stuck, but you do not want to downclimb the thin, slabby terrain.

Seated in a crack system, your buddies allowed some of the rope coils to drop below into a deep crack right underneath them. A few of the rope sections doubled back on themselves and are now tightly pinched off deep in the slot. They are unable to slide their hands into the tapered crack. The rope will not budge and there is no more slack to feed out despite your uncomfortable stance. What will you do, what can you advise your friends to do, and how could you have avoided this situation?

SOLUTION

Cleaning tools do not have to be used only for artificial protection! Because you can access the rope from a variety of angles, a cleaning tool could be indispensable in this situation. Your friends can work on dislodging the rope with the cleaning tool, trying to pry the rope free.

Either take a deep breath, hold on, and hope your belayer can free the line, or begin downclimbing, preparing for a possible lead fall on the runout slab. Hopefully with the additional slack generated as you downclimb, your friends will be able to free the rope. If they are not able to free the rope, you can either continue downclimbing or stop at a solid piece of protection and clip in while they continue battling the rope.

If this scenario included only you and your belayer, it is important that the belayer knows how to safely get hands-free with a mule-overhand so that he is able to work on freeing the rope. In the worst-case scenario you will need to downclimb until there is enough slack available to lower you down to the anchor and lend a hand.

The munter mule with a carabiner bight clip for backup

POTENTIAL PITFALLS

Make sure your belayer isn't too distracted by the rope-freeing process and is still providing you with a good belay.

PREVENTION

The best solution to this predicament runs along the lines of, "An ounce of prevention is worth a pound of pain." Rope management is often a difficult, overwhelming task for new climbers, and they do not realize how easily tangles and knots can happen. Do yourself the favor of setting yourself and your partners up for success by keeping belay ropes organized. At a crowded belay station or spots with deep cracks, take the time to make hanging holsters that ropes can feed in and out of, or designate good spots to stack the rope. Educate your climbing partners about the importance of good rope management and active belaying. It helps everyone in the long run.

SKILLS TO REVIEW

Mule overhand (chapter 2), getting hands-free (chapter 3)

SCENARIO 15

You and your partner are one double rope rappel away from getting off your climb. Your partner threads one end of the line through the rap chains. Once she has coiled one of the ropes in her hand, she tosses it down while simultaneously you continue pulling the second rope down from above. Unfortunately, she throws the rope directly into a tree below and the rope snags in its branches. She tugs and tugs, but the rope is caught beyond recovery. Meanwhile, you have run into a snag of your own; the rope you have been pulling on appears to be stuck above, caught on one of the route's many chicken heads. You have tried every trick you can think of for freeing the rope from below (swinging the rope out, flicking it, pulling from a different angle, etc.) to no avail. With both of your ropes stuck, how will you and your partner get down?

SOLUTION

Unfortunately, your partner's efforts at efficiency will end up costing time in the long run. Fix the ropes to the anchor. Have your partner slowly rappel the single strand using a third hand as a backup, taking care *not* to rappel below the tree. As soon as she is right above the tree (or can't rappel any lower without risking dropping below the tree), she can begin untangling the rope and pulling it up. A third-hand backup becomes very important so that she can keep her hands free for working on the rope.

Once the rope is untangled, she rappels all the way to the ground where she then reties in to the rope and reclimbs the pitch while you belay from above (or she ascends the line with an ascension rig).

Back at the anchor, she clips in, unties, and gives her end of the rope to you. You tie in and now, with her belaying, lead the pitch above. When you get to the stuck section of rope, either free it and toss it down to your partner and download, or continue up to the anchors, dragging the second rope with you, and rappel, hoping the rope will not snag again when you pull it.

POTENTIAL PITFALLS

If for some reason your partner could not climb the pitch back up to you (rappel routes do not always follow climbable lines), she would have to get out her waist and foot Prusiks and ascend the line she just rappelled.

If for some reason the section where the rope is stuck above is unclimbable, unaidable, and so on, you can still descend. Since you are just one rope length from the ground, you can fix one end of the rope to the anchor and rappel to the ground on that single strand.

PREVENTION

Good rope management (i.e., thinking about the obstacles below before throwing) may have avoided this predicament.

SKILLS TO REVIEW

Third-hand backup (chapter 4), French-freeing, tying an ascension rig and ascending a fixed line (chapter 5)

"Old school" techniques can add a quick safety margin in unexpected terrain.

SCENARIO 16

While leading out a long horizontal traverse on a desert tower, your partner falls, pen-duluming approximately 60 feet across the blank wall. The two of you are three pitches up; he had placed a #4 Camelot at the beginning of the traverse, then 15 feet later clipped an old piton that pulled out from the force of his fall. In his fall he hits a small ledge, shat-tering both ankles. He is now hanging approximately 10 feet to the right of you (the #4 Camelot holding his weight) and 60 feet below on the relatively blank wall. How can you assist him while taking care to attend to the possibility of a spinal injury incurred from the impact?

You have a spare line with you for the descent, which is several double-rope rappels.

SOLUTIONS

Since the only way out is to return to the base of the tower, set up a counterbalance rappel off of your partner's #4 Camelot. Clip the main rope to the belay anchor as a backup to the high piece. (Try to extend the anchor: you will want the extra slack for swinging toward your partner.) Make sure to put a third-hand backup on your rappel. Begin rappelling with all available gear (other than the pieces in the anchor and the #4). After rappelling about 20 feet, pendulum over to your partner's line and clip a bight of the second rope to his line. Return to your descent path, holding the rest of the spare rope. Then continue descending about 60 feet, until you are just across from your partner, about 15 feet away.

Build an anchor and pull your partner over with the spare line that is clipped to his line. Make a rescue spider and transfer onto the new anchor with a releasable hitch (MMO). You want him to be on a releasable hitch since you will have to get him back off the anchor to continue rappelling. Due to his broken ankles he is unable to stand (or climb) and unweight the anchor.

Now attend to his injuries, improvising a chest harness and using a shirt and some gear to provide splint support for his ankles. Pull the ropes and set up a double-rope tan-dem rappel. Set another anchor and repeat the process until you reach the ground. Each time you must transfer your partner onto the anchor with a releasable hitch. Once on the ground you need to take time to provide first aid for your partner, making sure he is stable before going for help with evacuation or attempting it yourself. If you suspect a spinal injury, you should find a backboard.

If your partner is in a life-threatening situation, and a counterbalance rappel is not fresh in your mind, consider escaping the belay and using the second rope to rap to your partner to provide life support and stabilization. Pendulum to find a good anchor and try to transfer your partner to it (this transfer might be hard if the anchor is significantly below or above him). Then ascend back to the anchor and clean up the system, pull his rope, and rappel back down on the original anchor. Continue down by tandem rappelling.

Speedy but thoughtful rope work will get you out of a jam.

POTENTIAL PITFALLS

Lots of course! Watch that #4. You are relying on only one piece of gear that has been fallen on and not reinspected. If you have any doubts, you must escape the belay, ascend to the piece, and back it up with any available gear. Unfortunately, your leader has the rack. It might be possible to remove the original anchor on the counterbalance descent.

PREVENTION

More solid pieces in the traverse. You should always protect against a bad pendulum.

SKILLS TO REVIEW

Munter-mule-overhand (chapter 2); counterbalance rappelling, tandem rappelling, and rescue spider (chapter 4); rigging an injured climber (chapter 4); ascending a fixed line (chapter 5)

SCENARIO 17

You are leading the last pitch of a five-pitch sport route. This pitch is tougher than you anticipated and you are spent! You've got three more bolts to go till the anchor but you've already spent a good fifteen minutes trying to advance to the next bolt. This pitch is beyond your partner's leading ability so lowering and offering him a shot at the section is not an option. Rappelling down the entire route is an option but you decide against it since the top of the climb is so close. Unfortunately, because this is a sport route you did not bring any sort of cordelette or rescue loops. How can you ascend up past the final three bolts to the anchor?

SOLUTION

Here's a handy trick for improvised aiding on a sport climb when you are without any tools (e.g. rescue loops, additional cordelette, etc.). Clip your remaining quickdraws together to create a long chain. Clip the last carabiner on one end of the chain around the draw (just the "dogbone" section of material) linked above. Insert your foot and stand up in the loop you've created and reach for the next bolt. Hopefully this will give you enough reach!

POTENTIAL PITFALLS

If you still can't reach, play with the length of the chain of quickdraws. The shorter the chain is the higher you can stand but the more difficult it may be to maintain your balance while transitioning to this position. Use the rock as much as you can to assist. Watch that the carabiner gates aren't pushed open depending on how you orient the chain.

PREVENTION

Considering this is a multipitch, you should have brought some extra cord and rescue loops along, regardless of the fact that it is a sport route.

SKILLS TO REVIEW

This is a variation on French-freeing (chapter 5).

SCENARIO 18

You and your teammates are crossing a glacier in two rope teams of two, with each person carrying a coiled portion of rope, when your partner, who is breaking trail for the group, punches through a snow bridge. You are able to arrest the fall and build an anchor. Upon arrival at the crevasse lip, you realize it is extremely undercut and the climbing rope has sliced several feet deep through the lip, leaving your partner choked up against the lip's underbelly. How will you get your partner out? What can he do to help the situation?

SOLUTION:

Prepare another lip off to the side where the rope cuts into the original lip. Remove as much snow as you can but try not to dislodge the snow above the climber if possible. Bring the second team up to your anchor (make sure it's probed and free of crevasses), and have them untie and attach one end of their rope to the anchor. Drop a bight with a carabiner down to your partner, have him clip in to a 2:1 system and haul him out. Once he is clipped in and moving on the 2:1, he can unclip from the main climbing rope if it is hopelessly stuck in the original lip.

POTENTIAL PITFALLS

A huge snow plug (created by the rope slicing vertically from the fall and then horizontally as the climber moves to the new rope) dropping on the climber would be bad. Speed and good systems will help get him out of there fast. Do not just pull him up into the original lip; you will need to prep another site in this situation.

PREVENTION

Crevasse falls are part of the risk of traveling through glaciated terrain. There are of course several measures that can be taken to improve your chances of safe travel: using a probe, receiving a more formal belay, and/or crawling on all fours over suspicious snow bridges. If you find yourself punching through consistently, it is important to consider if it is really appropriate to be traveling in crevasse country in such conditions. Should you be traveling instead at night, when it is cooler, or wait a day to see if conditions firm up?

SKILLS TO REVIEW

Raising systems (chapter 6)

SCENARIO 19

While leading the third pitch of a five-pitch ice climb, your partner takes a leader fall. She has dislocated her shoulder and is in extreme pain. She is unable to continue climbing. She has climbed 30 feet past the rope's halfway point. You have a second rope stacked beside you at the belay, a hanging belay of one V-thread and one ice screw. How will you safely assist your partner? What safety precautions should you keep in mind?

SOLUTIONS

Lower your partner to the lowest ice screw you can get her to where she can clip in (make sure the ice screw is a good one!). Escape the belay, moving the belay to the anchor. Because she has climbed approximately 30 feet beyond the halfway point, you should only need about 30 more feet of rope to get her to the anchor. If there is no low protection, you can tie on the other rope and pass the knot to lower her all the way to you at the anchor. Continue descending via rappels (tandem if necessary).

If there is a bit of low protection, you may need to rope-solo on the other rope to clean the bottom pieces and *then* pass the knot so that you will have enough space to lower her to your station before the knot hits the pro. Build a new anchor for this step if you have the materials.

The third option is to escape the belay and use the second rope to rope-solo up to her and start building your descent anchors there. Ice is nice in that you can generally build your anchors where you need them (obviously, depending on ice quality). You can then transfer onto a new anchor and clean the first one as you rappel by on the way down.

POTENTIAL PITFALLS

If your partner does not have a good quality screw to clip in to, then just escape the belay and keep her on your anchor and the screw she is hanging on already.

Do not start rope-soloing or ascending on her line; you have another rope available, so use it! With weight, ice anchors pressure-melt—not something to worry about in this scenario, but be careful leaving a patient hanging or attached to an ice anchor. Ice anchors will melt out over time, especially with a bit of weight.

Due to pressure-melt, rope soloing is preferable to ascending the fallen leader's line. Ascending her line would put more weight on the piece she is hanging from, thereby increasing the rate at which pressure-melting occurs.

PREVENTION

Careful on those ice leads! This scenario illustrates an advantage of climbing with two ropes (including double or twins).

SKILLS TO REVIEW

Escaping a belay (chapter 3), rope-soloing (chapter 5), passing a knot (chapter 7)

SCENARIO 20

You are cleaning a route led by your partner and arrive at a spot where the rope has doubled over on itself and is hopelessly stuck in the crack. You were climbing the route quickly, thereby generating pools of slack, and your belayer was having a hard time keeping up with you. You decide that the rope must have gotten stuck in one such instance. You work on the rope for a while without success. Given that your belayer can't pull in any more slack and is therefore unable to belay you, how can you safely continue up the line? First assume that you can communicate with your partner. What would you do differently if you could not communicate with your partner?

SOLUTION

Call up for your partner to escape the belay and fix the line. Meanwhile, you can pull out your rescue loops and a cordelette and fashion an ascension rig. Tie your ascension rig to the line with Prusik hitches. You will have to untie from the climbing rope once you are clipped in to your Prusiks. Because the rope is stuck, you will not have the option of clipping in short with an overhand or figure eight on a bight as a backup. Once you have confirmed that the line is fixed, begin ascending all the way to the anchor.

If you can't communicate with your partner, do the same thing.

It is up to you and your partner to decide what to do next. Perhaps she descends back down the line to give freeing the rope a shot. It is certainly worth giving it another try before cutting the line, which may be your next option. If you are short on materials for creating an ascension rig, don't forget about the Garda hitch!

POTENTIAL PITFALLS

If you have no means of creating an ascension rig, you might consider tying in above the stuck rope and then cutting the rope below your tie in as a last resort. This is not recommended if you will need the rope for your descent. If you have not been able to communicate with your belayer, be aware that the added force of your ascending may take her by surprise.

PREVENTION

It is important for a variety of reasons not to generate much slack as a follower: the potential of shock loading the anchor should you take a big fall, the chance of ropes getting stuck as in this scenario, and so on. As a follower it is your responsibility to keep appropriate rope tension and communicate with your belayer.

SKILLS TO REVIEW

Tying a Purcell Prusik (chapter 4), ascension rig, ascending a fixed line and backing up a fixed line, and ascending with a Garda hitch (chapter 5)

SCENARIO 21

While leading a pitch, your partner falls and does not want to continue. She calls down to be lowered. She has only used about a third of the rope, so rope length will not be a problem. However, the anchor from which you are belaying is located off to the side of the climb and under a large roof. How will you get your partner back to the belay anchor once she is lowered past the roof? What different steps would you take if she were knocked unconscious and unable to help?

SOLUTIONS

For the conscious patient, your partner could clip a quickdraw to the rope (or simply pull hand-over-hand) which would keep her close to the wall as she lowers. She would have to clip around or through each piece of gear she passed. Another option: lower her down to where you can talk and see each other. Get hands-free from the belay. Get a bight of rope or long cord (made into a sling) and throw it to her. Alternately, she can throw you something (like a chain of runners girth-hitched together) to clip to the anchor. Attach the rope bight or sling to both the anchor and your partner. Continue lowering her and have her pull herself to the anchor. If she is unable to pull in, just lower her until she swings in due to the tether attaching her to the anchor, and then bring her up to the anchor.

If your partner is unconscious or none of the above options works, you will need to get a sling on her somehow. There are a couple of options, but first get hands-free. Option one: Take a carabiner and tape open the gate. Add some webbing and see if you can lasso the lass. Option two: Escape the belay. Rope-solo or ascend out to where you can attach a tether to her or her rope. You may have to go up a ways if she is really hanging in space. This is assuming you want to get her back to your anchor. If she is unconscious you may need to ascend to her and administer care. Your subsequent steps will be very situation-dependent. Choose the option that will get you to your unconscious partner most quickly.

POTENTIAL PITFALLS

Take care not to hurt your partner with the carabiner toss method. If your partner is conscious, try to use a rope section or cord to tether her to the anchor; webbing has less give. If she becomes unable to pull in on the webbing, she will have quite a bit of force as she swings back out against it. You could generate a very large outward shock load on your anchor this way.

PREVENTION

Be careful where you put the belay anchor. If it is possible to put it lower and not wedge yourself up under a roof, that is generally better.

SKILLS TO REVIEW

Escaping a belay (chapter 3), rope soloing (chapter 5)

SCENARIO 22

You are belaying at the top of a two-pitch trad-route tower. Your inexperienced partner is out of sight about two-thirds of the way up the pitch. He allows his rope to get caught on a rock nubbin as he climbs up and sideways, generating about 6 feet of slack. At this point he falls and swings into a small dihedral and smacks his head. You feel the sudden large fall and can get no response from him. You have only one rope because the tower has two single-rope raps to get off the other side. What will you do?

SOLUTION

Begin a counterbalance rappel. Take all the gear except the anchor with you. Descend to your partner and set a new anchor. Transfer him to the anchor with a releasable hitch and attend to life support. Set a single-rope rappel and continue tandem rappelling until reaching the ground.

POTENTIAL PITFALLS

Depending on how you as the belayer are situated at the top anchor, it could be tough to quickly switch into a counterbalance rappel; this will be situation-dependent.

PREVENTION

When following, be careful when you choose to climb above your belay line.

SKILLS TO REVIEW

Counterbalance rappelling and tandem rappelling (chapter 4)

SCENARIO 23

You are traveling in the middle on a rope team of three through heavily crevassed terrain. Snow conditions are not good; you and your teammates have been popping through snow bridges all day. Suddenly, Adam, located at the front of the line, takes a long fall, deep into a crevasse. You need to establish communication with Adam but there is another obvious snow bridge between you and the point where he fell in—the same snow bridge that Adam's foot popped through only minutes ago.

A few questions to think about: Considering the precarious nature of the terrain between you and Adam, is it still necessary to approach the lip of the crevasse? If so, how will you safely do so? How will you proceed from there?

SOLUTION

Unless you are able to establish verbal communication with Adam by shouting, it is necessary to approach the crevasse to assess the extent of his fall and the nature of his injuries (if any). Considering the lousy snowpack, it is likely that Adam's rope has cut (potentially quite deeply) through the crevasse's lip and you will need to prep the lip for him.

The first thing for you to do is to establish an anchor near the middle person, as that person continues holding Adam. Then belay yourself off the anchor toward Adam. Make yourself as light as possible as you approach Adam, ditching your backpack, etc. Crawl on all fours to distribute your weight as much as possible. Have your ascension rig already set on the line, sliding it alongside you as you move out, as a belay. Probe the snow bridge before getting onto it; consider trying an alternative route if the line Adam took does not look so good.

Once you reach the lip of the crevasse, assess Adam's condition and make a plan. Can he ascend on his own, or does he need assistance? If he needs assistance, then your third will need to come forward so you can use her portion of the rope for creating a raising system. Decide if you need to pad the lip, to what extent, or if Adam needs an entirely new line sent down and if that is possible or not.

POTENTIAL PITFALLS

The biggest risk is more snow bridges giving out as you approach Adam.

PREVENTION

Crevasse falls are part of the risk of traveling through glaciated terrain. There are of course several measures that can be taken to improve your chances of safe travel: using a probe, receiving a more formal belay and/or crawling on all fours over suspicious snow bridges. and so on. If you find yourself punching through consistently, it is important to consider

Nothing like a little crevasse rescue and fixed line ascension practice to keep your skills fresh.

if it is really appropriate to be traveling in crevasse country in such conditions. Should you be traveling instead at night, when it is cooler, or wait a day to see if conditions firm up?

SKILLS TO REVIEW
Ascending a fixed line (chapter 5), raising systems (chapter 6)

SCENARIO 24

You are belaying your partner on the first pitch of a multipitch sport route when she takes a lead fall just 10 feet from the top anchor. Both of her ankles have been injured in the fall, and she is unable to continue climbing. All you have left on the ground is about 20 feet of rope—not enough to lower your partner back to the ground. Because this is a route with a walk-off descent, there was no need for a second rope for rappelling. You did not build a ground anchor beforehand and there is nothing in the immediate vicinity. All you have is one cordelette and a locking carabiner. How will you help your partner? (She does not have any rescue knowledge.)

SOLUTIONS

If the upper piece is a good bolt, consider lowering your partner with whatever amount of rope you have left. You can then start climbing (or ascending) up. She will start to lower. As you go up, remove the quickdraws. When you pass her—if you are close enough—attach a rescue loop to her line and clip it to your harness. This will be a safety backup for you when she gets to the ground. Ideally, when she reaches the ground there will still be two or three draws between you.

Once she is on the ground, you have a few options. You can clip in to the nearest bolt, attach the rope, and rappel the line back to your partner, leaving the line fixed. Or you can have your partner untie. (Careful! Make sure you are clipped to a bolt or have a Prusik connecting you to her line as previously described; otherwise, you'll be dropped. Even the ropes out through the last draw and rappel the line. Near the end of the rappel, clip a draw in to each of two bolts (you'll have to reach up high to a bolt above to do this), and clip one side of the rope through both draws. Clip yourself to one of the bolts and pull the rope so that it stays through two draws (this can be done off one bolt, but it is good to realize that you can do it off a couple bolts as described here); do another single-rope rappel, hopefully to the ground. Repeat if you need to. You now have your hurt leader on the ground and your rope for carrying her if necessary.

You have another option at the moment when you pass your partner as you are climbing up. Switch to a tandem rappel, but make sure that both of your body weights are not just hanging and rapping off of one bolt.

Alternatively, you could lower her to the nearest bolt, have her clip in and fix the line to the bolt. You would then ascend up to her. However, this process will take longer than the one described above so it's not the best option if getting her down to the ground as quickly as possible is critical.

POTENTIAL PITFALLS

Back up single bolts whenever and however possible. In many cases single bolts should not be trusted. Be careful as you go up the route to maintain your status as rescuer. You do not want to turn into a victim or get stuck at the top of the climb where you are no longer able to help your partner.

PREVENTION

Consider the consequences if you forego building a ground anchor even at a sport crag.

SKILLS TO REVIEW

Rappelling, counterbalance rappelling, and tandem rappelling (chapter 4)

SCENARIO 25

While cleaning the last pitch of an eight-pitch route, your partner is struck by a rock and is seriously injured, floating in and out of consciousness. For a variety of reasons it makes more sense for you to evacuate him via the top of the route instead of rappelling all the way back down; there is an access road leading to the top of the cliff, with a large cleared parking area (if a helicopter landing is needed). You are also looking at rappelling eight full rope lengths versus hauling him 30 feet up. Your partner is trailing the second rope. How will you get your partner to safety?

SOLUTION

Your partner's injuries must first be assessed. If he is only 30 feet away, you may be able to do an effective job of assessment from where you are. But if you can't see him, you will have to get down to him to administer first aid. The easiest way to do this is to fix the brake strand to the anchor and rappel down to him on the single fixed line; then ascend back up once you have assessed and treated him.

Assuming he does not need any support slings (provide them if necessary), it is time to start raising. Build your raising system. If your partner is conscious enough, a 2:1 drop loop assist may be a viable option. If he is not conscious enough to clip in to the carabiner, you will need to build at least a 3:1.

POTENTIAL PITFALLS

Considering that your partner is trailing the second rope, take great care if you notice any increase in resistance in your system. An increase in resistance could indicate that something is snagged. If that occurs you will have to descend to your partner and attempt to free the rope. Ideally, you will take the second rope from him when you descend to administer care.

PREVENTION

Rockfall is one of the risks inherent to rock climbing.

SKILLS TO REVIEW

Escaping a belay (chapter 3), rappelling, rigging an injured climber (chapter 4), 2:1 and 3:1 raising systems (chapter 6)

SCENARIO 26

While exiting out a large roof on lead, your partner falls and takes a long whipper into space. She is uninjured and raring to go. But she is hanging in midair. How can you work together to get her back up into the crack? Because she was a bit run out when she fell, she is unable to reach up to the rock or to any of her pieces. She has traveled past the rope's halfway point, so lowering her down is not an option.

SOLUTION

There are multiple options, ranging from the easy to the more complex. Easiest is the "bounce technique." She grabs the rope above her and pulls up hand-over-hand. At the same time you lock off your belay device and put all your weight on the rope. She lets go and you drop a couple feet while she remains slightly higher than she was. Repeat. She could also ascend up the line back to the roof using either an improvised ascension rig or a foot loop and Garda hitch. Finally, as the belayer you could build a 3:1 raising system off your harness and haul her back up the remaining feet to the roof.

POTENTIAL PITFALLS

Make sure your gear is strong and secure. The first technique can put a lot of force on pieces. The solutions range from the most work-intensive for the climber and least time-consuming to the most work-intensive for the belayer and most time-consuming.

PREVENTION

That's the way roofs go. Hopefully she will work on getting bomber gear placements with better spacing (less runout) and not rule out the possibility of using some points of aid through the roof if need be.

SKILLS TO REVIEW

Ascending a fixed line (chapter 5) and raising systems (chapter 6)

SCENARIO 27

You and your partner are climbing at an infrequently visited choss pile. The rock is loose, the cracks are flared and dirty, but you love a good adventure. You are at the top of the route's final pitch when your partner (who is cleaning the route) pulls off a rock that smashes right down on her hand and knee. She can't continue climbing and asks for a raise. She is just 40 feet from the top; you have plenty of rope at your disposal. But you are nervous about your anchor; the rock quality is not good and you have both been choosing to belay off your body for the entire climb to lessen forces on the anchor pieces. You are concerned about the ability of your current anchor to hold the additional forces that a raising system will generate. What are your options for raising your partner and what can you do to make the situation as safe as possible?

SOLUTION

Do your best to reinforce your anchor. Add as many additional pieces to the anchor as you think necessary. You could also try introducing more material into the system to favor your strongest and most secure pieces.

    If you are still hesitant to set up a full raising system on your anchor, even with reinforcement, you do have a few options, but you must have a good belay position to execute them. See if you can talk your partner into ascending up the line with an improvised ascension rig using her uninjured limbs. If she agrees to ascend, tie off the belay with a mule-overhand and brace yourself. If she does not want to ascend, then you can build a quick 3:1 right off your harness. Again, make sure you have a good stance and are secured on your anchor if you attempt this option.

POTENTIAL PITFALLS

If there is a large weight differential between you and your partner, then holding her weight while she ascends or hauling her off your harness will be *very* difficult and somewhat painful.

PREVENTION

If the rock is that dangerous, do you really want to be climbing there in the first place? If the answer is still yes, try to stick to routes with good anchors.

SKILLS TO REVIEW

Mule-overhand (chapter 2), anchor-building techniques (chapter 4), ascending a fixed line (chapter 5), raising systems (chapter 6)

While leading an upward traversing pitch your partner takes a hard fall and dislocates her shoulder. The rock quality has been very poor all along and the climbing more difficult than expected. There is not enough rope available to lower her and there is no way to reach over to her either; she is approximately 160 feet out, 50 feet over and hanging 5 feet below her last piece; a blue TCU. She is in great pain and is asking for assistance. The descent is three single-rope rappels. What is your plan of action?

SOLUTION

As described in "Ascending to a Hurt Leader" you will need to reinforce the bottom anchor as best you can, escape the belay, and begin ascending the rope. Keep your fingers crossed that the blue TCU holds. Selectively clean some gear as you go to use in reinforcing the top anchor. Do your best to build an anchor where your partner is hanging. Transfer your partner to the new anchor and clean the upper TCU if you can. Fix the climbing rope to the new anchor. Next descend back down to your original belay anchor, free the rope, and dismantle the anchor. Time then to re-ascend to your partner, cleaning the route as you go. Once you arrive back at your partner rig the anchor for a tandem rappel and start heading down.

POTENTIAL PITFALLS

If the small TCU blows you both will go for a little ride. There is always the chance that you will not be able to set an anchor at the site where your partner has fallen. See the next scenario for ways to deal with that predicament.

PREVENTION

Injury is a risk inherent to rock climbing. Contributing factors may have been poor rock quality and/or exceeding abilities.

SKILLS TO REVIEW

Belay escapes (chapter 2), ascending to a hurt leader (chapter 5)

SCENARIO 29

Now, using the circumstances described in Scenario 28, what would you do if your partner has fallen twenty feet below her last piece and is hanging in space next to a section of blank rock where there is no spot to build an anchor? She is still asking for you to help reduce her shoulder pain.

SOLUTION

Create a good anchor at your partner's last (highest) piece of gear. Then descend and attend to your partner's needs. Once she is stable (or as close to it as you can get her), take all

Groups are able to handle larger challenges.

the gear from her, hit reverse, and move back up the line to the top anchor. Clip yourself in to the anchor and build a raising system (improvise with slings as the haul strands). Raise your partner to the anchor and attach her with a releasable hitch. Make sure the climbing rope is attached to the top anchor. Either rappel on the single strand or descend back down to your original anchor, clean it, and then ascend back up to your new anchor, cleaning gear as you go. Begin tandem rappels.

There are other possible solutions depending on the actual configuration of the climb and anchoring options.

POTENTIAL PITFALLS

You will need to be fast and creative with your anchoring and ascending systems. Make sure you maintain good pieces securing the rope system. Be careful not to clean too many pieces for use in building the top anchor.

PREVENTION

Same as Scenario 28.

SKILLS TO REVIEW

Belay escapes (chapter 2), ascending to a hurt leader (chapter 5), raising systems (Chapter 6)

CHAPTER 9

Early morning helicopter in the wilderness

Getting Outside Help

Sometimes self-rescue is not an option or is only part of what a situation calls for. This chapter addresses what is involved in calling for outside help. As the party requesting rescue it is important to be realistic in your expectations of what rescuers can do to help you. They will be working under the same limiting factors you are: terrain, weather, and darkness to name a few. All of the rescue situations discussed in this chapter provide basic guidelines and suggestions. Every climbing area (be it a crag or mountain range) has its own unique protocol and resources.

DECISION-MAKING TECHNIQUES AND TIPS

Rescue decisions are important, stressful, and tricky. The best solution is not always obvious and the difficulties surrounding decision-making typically are compounded by the distraction of an emotional situation. To look at decision-making, we will focus on three situations: one rescuer and one responsive patient, one rescuer and one unresponsive patient, and lastly, more than one rescuer and a responsive patient.

The first step in any emergency decision-making process is to breathe; or, in the words of Teton pioneer Paul Petzoldt, "Smoke a butt." Take a moment to clear your head and take full stock of the situation. In only a few circumstances will those extra minutes be detrimental. Taking that time to think can be difficult; all your instincts may be urging you to "Act now!" But poorly concocted plans can often result in time wasted in the long run or in more injuries.

After working through the initial emergency procedures (chapter 2), the first plan of action should be to get your patient up or down the climb to a safe and protected spot accessible to rescuers, as long as that process will not make the patient's condition worse. This should be attempted only if it is reasonable for you as a solo rescuer to move the patient.

With a responsive patient. A solo rescuer can often get good advice and can actually help calm the patient by involving him in some of the planning and decisions. This is not always the case, but it should definitely be considered. By involving the patient in simple, relevant decisions, it is possible to see if he will be able to have a role with bigger-picture issues. For example: if the patient is giving good information while you are re-positioning his broken limb and is indicating in what position he is most comfortable, you may want to discuss how you are going to get him out of there. Listening to the patient's input, even if he is quite injured, can be good for both of you. The patient will generally be supportive of your efforts and will better understand the plan if he helps make it. You get a second opinion and sometimes new ideas, given your patient's closeness to the challenge ahead. However, involving your patient in rescue decisions is not always the best idea—for instance, if you know the patient's stress level will rise due to uncertainties or if the patient does not perceive the severity of his injuries or situation.

You may or may not need to leave a responsive patient; following are some considerations should this be necessary.

With an unresponsive patient. The solo rescuer must rely on his or her own judgment and decisions. An unresponsive patient in the backcountry is likely to be severely injured. Good first-aid skills must be used with this patient.

Most likely, you will need to make a decision at some point about leaving an unresponsive patient to get more help. Remember that environmental conditions may change while you are gone: shade becomes sun, sun becomes rain or snow, and so on. Prepare and situate the patient for these possibilities if you can by insulating him with padding below and layers on top. Regardless of the air temperature, the patient's body temperature will cool down. It is also possible that the patient could resume consciousness while you are away. Leave him a message and supplies that will help him: water, basic food, and easily accessible clothing. Do not leave him with gear he does not know how to use, with complex foods, or with prescription drugs he could overdose on or have an allergy to. If the patient is unconscious, it is vital that he be left in the recovery position.

There is no point leaving your patient if you do not have a plan, so know the

WATCH WHAT YOU SAY

Medical professionals say that a person's hearing is the last thing to go. Be aware of this as a rescuer; even if your patient is unresponsive, reassuring and encouraging him can make a difference. Tell him what you are doing and always encourage him. Also, be sensitive in your language and the manner in which you describe your patient's condition.

following before you depart:

- The patient's exact location so you can find him again, as well as so you can describe the location to others (mark coordinates on a map or write down a description; in times of high stress it becomes easy to confuse details)
- Where you are going and how long you think you will be gone
- What condition the patient is in when you leave relative to when you started care
- What help you need from the other rescuers (horse, helicopter, oxygen, etc.)

When there is more than one rescuer. Communication becomes paramount. Many hands can make light work, but only if there is a brain controlling them well. It is best to have one lead rescuer in this situation. If possible, the lead rescuer should not be the primary caregiver. It is hard to both keep tabs on the big picture and provide direct patient care. If you have the resources, it is best to put a knowledgeable first-aider in charge of the patient and have another leader direct the rescue. You may be in a situation that the best person for both tasks is the same individual. In this case, focus on stabilizing the patient, and then train someone else to step in and take on patient care while the person most qualified for both roles steps out to be the lead rescuer.

The lead rescuer should keep the other rescuers occupied and productive. Some jobs may seem unnecessary, but in a rescue situation people like to feel like they are helping out; keeping people busy also can help keep their minds off the severity of the situation and focused on the task at hand. If there are excess hands, put them to work. Have people gather firewood, set up tents, make hot water, build anchors, coil ropes, scout the route down, and so on. Keep people busy but, as lead rescuer, try not to add too much unnecessary supervision to your list of tasks; keep your priorities in focus.

The "after" of a rescue is an aspect often overlooked. Everyone's combination of climbing and life experience varies greatly. Rescues affect everyone differently, whether the circumstances were traumatic

POST-TRAUMATIC STRESS DISORDER

According to the National Mental Health Organization and the National Institute for Mental Health, the following symptoms experienced more than a month after a particular event are indicative of post-traumatic stress disorder (PTSD): reexperiencing the incident in the form of flashbacks, nightmares, or frightening thoughts, especially when exposed to similar circumstances or surroundings. Anniversaries of the event can also trigger these responses. People experiencing post-traumatic stress disorder may also have emotional trouble, sleep disturbances, depression, irritability, anger, anxiety, or guilt. See appendix D, Continuing Education, and appendix E, Recommended Reading, for resources for identifying and coping with PTSD.

or trite. It is important to discuss the rescue as a group after it is complete and seek professional help if necessary.

CARRYING DEVICES AND LITTERS

So you have gotten yourself safely off the wall, out of the crevasse, or down the frozen waterfall, now what? Below are several improvised carrying devices to help get you the rest of the way out. Ideally, the injured party can walk out on his own. If that is not possible, the severity of his injuries will determine how much assistance he needs. We have described the carrying methods we find to be the most practical; other methods do, of course, exist.

Keep in mind that the following information excludes any assessment for spinal injuries. If spinal injury is suspected, it may make more sense to go for help rather than trying to evacuate the patient yourself, risking further injury: spinal injury is not something to mess around with, especially if you lack specific wilderness medical training. See the Continuing Education and Recommended Reading appendixes for more information on wilderness first aid.

Realize that carrying a patient will be a difficult and physically demanding process no matter how you slice it, especially if the patient is significantly larger than you. Although we advocate self-sufficiency and resourcefulness, trying to carry another person can be an easy way to end up with two injured people instead of just one. In this situation it may make more sense to get additional help, either from bystanders or trained personnel.

ONE- AND TWO-PERSON CARRIES

Here are a few options for carrying a person out by yourself or with a partner. Do what you can to pad yourself and your patient from materials cutting into skin, particularly if this is going to be a long evacuation. The different ways of carrying presented use different materials, thereby allowing you to improvise appropriately based on the resources you have.

One-Person Split-Rope Carry

1. Coil the entire climbing rope into a mountaineer's coil sized normally for wearing slung across your torso. Tie it off as normal.
2. Halve the coils into two equal sections.
3. Have your patient step into the loops, one foot into each section. Have her pull the coils up (like putting on a pair of pants) until the coils rest right below her crotch. The wraps of the mountaineer's coil should be resting on her lower back.
4. Now insert your arms into the upper section of the coil's loops (one arm through each side), like you are putting on a backpack, your back to your patient's belly (fig. 9-1). If possible, have your patient situate herself on an elevated surface like a boulder or a fallen tree. This will make the lifting process significantly easier for you.

Useful Variations

You may find it more comfortable to attach some sort of chest strap across the mountaineer's coil. Here is one way to do it:

1. Girth-hitch a runner around one side of the coil.
2. Bring it across your chest, around the other coil, and back to the side you started from.
3. Tie the runner off using a simple and easily releasable knot, like a double half hitch.

If your partner's mental status is unreliable, you may want to secure her upper body to you. The coil carry described above relies on the patient's ability to hold on to keep from tilting backward.

1. Loop a long runner over your patient's back, snugging it up under her armpits.
2. Tie the runner off in front, over your chest.

One-Person Backpack Carry

Some full-size backpacks have zippers running the pack's entire length on each side. These zippers can be used for more than just packing; they serve a useful rescue purpose too.

1. Stuff the bottom one-quarter of the backpack with soft padding like extra jackets and down. (Nothing too heavy—remember you are carrying all of this.)
2. Unzip both side zippers all the way down.
3. Have the patient step into the backpack, inserting his legs through the

Fig. 9-1. One-person split-rope carry. The patient puts her legs through the loops of the split mountaineer's coil. The rescuer then inserts his arms through the coil's loops as if he were putting on a backpack.

openings created by the unzipped zippers. (Most people prefer riding piggyback style versus back to back.)

4. The patient pulls the backpack up to crotch level.

5. Taking great care to not injure your back, put the backpack on your back and stand up. (Again, try to situate the patient on something at your torso height to make picking up the load easier.)

Two-Person Split-Rope Carry

1. Split your rope in a mountaineer's coil but make the coils approximately 3 feet in diameter.

2. Each rescuer slings one side of the divided coil across her torso, just like a gear sling.

3. The patient sits on the wrapped portion, supporting himself with his arms around his rescuers' shoulders. His rescuers cross their inside arms to provide additional support for his back.

Two-Person Pole Carry

Each rescuer will need two double-length runners.

1. Each rescuer puts a runner on in gear-sling fashion, running from one shoulder to the far hip.

2. Each rescuer repeats step 1 on the opposite shoulder. The two runners should form an X across each rescuer's body.

3. Find a long branch approximately 6 to 8 feet in length. (Extended telescopic

ski poles doubled up, or stick clips duct-taped or lashed together with multiple clove hitches may work too.)

4. Insert the branch through the bottom of all four runners, creating a railing for the patient between you and the other rescuer.

5. The patient sits on the rail (she'll certainly appreciate padding), her arms around the shoulders of each rescuer while the two rescuers link arms behind her to provide additional stability.

IMPROVISED STRETCHERS

If your patient is severely injured you may need to evacuate him on a stretcher. Obviously, a manufactured backboard is ideal, however here are some improvisational options. First described are stretchers that could be carried by just two people (depending, of course, on weight and size of the patient and rescuers). Described last are stretchers that depend upon the power of more than just two rescuers.

Jacket Stretcher

You will need two long poles (branches, skis, etc.), approximately 3 feet longer than the height of your patient, and at least three to four upper-body layers. The tougher the fabric (i.e., less stretchy) the better.

1. Slide the poles down inside the torso of the layers.

2. Evenly space the layers down the length of the poles. The more layers you can spare, the better; the fewer the layers, the more your patient's

weight will droop and sag in the stretcher.

3. Aim for about 1.5 feet of excess pole on either end of the stretcher to give yourself enough room to carry.

4. Consider adding stabilizers (improvise with tree branches, telescopic poles, backpack stays, etc.) at either end of the stretcher to help maintain the stretcher's integrity as you carry your patient. (See fig. 9-2)

5. One rescuer carries the litter at each end. Be careful of the terrain you try to cross; if you drop your patient there is nothing protecting his back.

Rope-Bed Stretcher

Again, you will need two poles (as described for the jacket stretcher, above), but this time you will form the stretcher's surface out of climbing rope.

1. Lay the two poles on the ground parallel to each other, no wider than the width of your patient's body. (If the stretcher is too wide your patient will sag and swing, making the stretcher more difficult for you to carry and much more uncomfortable for her.)

2. Tie one end of the rope off to one end of one of the poles.

3. Bring the rope over to the parallel pole and tie it off with a clove hitch, making sure to keep appropriate stretcher width in mind.

4. Cross back over to the other side and tie the rope off with a clove hitch.

5. Repeat steps 3 and 4 several times.

Eventually you will have to slide your series of clove hitches along the pole to make room for more hitches.

6. Continue until you have created a diagonal matt of rope running the length of the stretcher, leaving 1.5 feet of room at each end for carrying. (See fig. 9-2.)

The more rungs of rope you provide your patient, the more comfortable and stable her ride will be. As a minimum guideline, rope rungs should be no more than 6 inches apart.

If possible, pad the stretcher bed with clothing or empty backpacks. This will make it a much more comfortable ride. (There is, however, a critical balance between your patient's comfort and the amount of weight you as a rescuer are carrying.) As with the jacket stretcher, consider adding stabilizers to either end of the stretcher to help it maintain its shape.

With either the jacket stretcher or the rope-bed stretcher, if your materials are sturdy enough, you *may* be able to drag the setup behind you. Make sure to create some sort of foot bar with webbing for your patient so that she does not slide right out of the stretcher as you pull it along. Depending on the terrain, consider securing her into the rig (not too tight)—again, to keep her from falling out.

Opposite: Fig. 9-2.
Top: Jacket stretcher;
Middle: Rope-bed stretcher;
Bottom: Sheet stretcher.

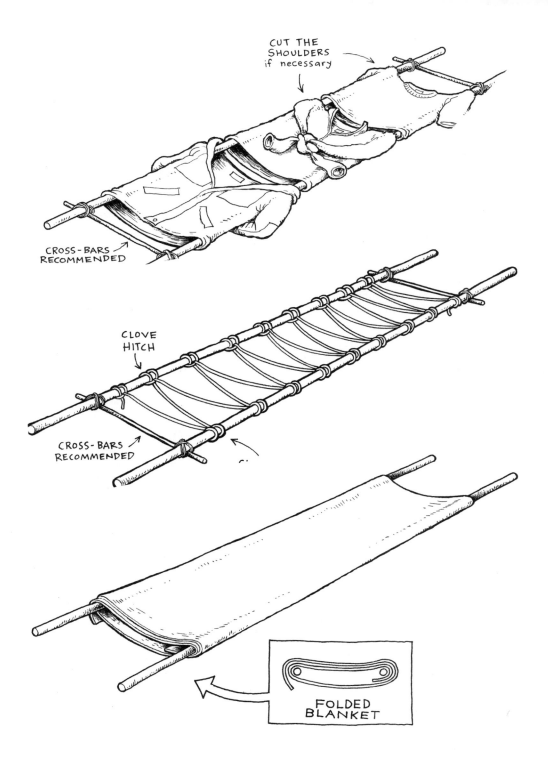

CUT THE
SHOULDERS
if necessary

CROSS-BARS
RECOMMENDED

CLOVE
HITCH

CROSS-BARS
RECOMMENDED

FOLDED
BLANKET

Sheet Stretcher

Once again you will need two poles (as described for the jacket stretcher, above). You will also need some sort of large sheet, like an unfurled large rope bag, a large tarp, a tent body, or tent fly.

1. Measure off three equal sections of the sheet right next to one another. The sections should be equal to the patient's body width and height. Any excess can be doubled up.
2. Lay the two poles on either side of the sheet's middle section, lengthwise.
3. One at a time, fold the two outside sections up over the top of the poles, one on top of the other. (See fig. 9-2.)

The patient's body weight will keep the sections from slipping out. But be careful, as the sections will begin to slip with time and jostling.

Climbing-Rope Stretcher

Unless the rescuers are significantly larger than the patient, this type of stretcher demands multiple carriers. You will need one climbing rope.

1. Find the rope's midpoint.
2. Starting at the midpoint, lay sixteen bights of rope out side by side in a continuous S pattern. The bights should be equal in length to your patient's body. Sixteen bights are a guideline; as with the rope-bed stretcher, the more rope rungs the better it supports your patient.
3. From the resulting stack of excess rope at either end of the row of bights, lay a length of rope on both sides parallel to the row of bights.
4. Insert the apex of the bight through the skeleton of a clove hitch (tied in the length of rope described as running parallel to the bights in step 3) and tighten (fig. 9-3). Aim for the resulting bight to be approximately 3 inches, uniform in size as you proceed down the line.
5. Work your way down the entire side, tying clove hitches and inserting the apex of every bight. (Hint: As you tighten each clove hitch down, try to minimize the amount of slack you create on the side of bights you have already tied; Try to bring slack down to the side you still have yet to tie clove hitches in. This will keep the stretcher tighter.)
6. Repeat on the other side.
7. Now thread the excess rope (that ran the length of the rows of bights) through the bights coming out of each clove hitch. Fig. 9-4 shows a rope stretcher completed to this point.
8. Continue threading around and around with each side of the rope.
9. When you come to the foot and head of the stretcher, wrap the rope around itself to keep the strands together. This will also make the stretcher easier to carry.
10. Repeat the threading process at least five or six times, or until you have used the entire rope.
11. Tie both sides off using any applicable knot.

Fig. 9-3. Climbing rope stretcher: Step 4. The apex of the bight is inserted into clove hitch.

As with the rope-bed stretcher, consider lining the stretcher bed. You must work backwards in deconstructing this stretcher; otherwise you'll end up with an absolute mess of rope.

Carabiner Alternative

Threading the rope through each bight multiple times is time-consuming, both in building and breaking down. You must deconstruct the stretcher just as you constructed it—otherwise you will end up with a massive tangle on your hands. This alternative requires multiple carabiners; although heavier because of the added metal, it is faster to make and much easier to undo.

1. Lay out the rope just as described above and lay a carabiner at the apex of each bight.

2. Like before, tie a clove hitch in the strand of rope running the length of the row of bights. Clip the carabiner into the clove hitch.
3. Insert the apex of the bight into the carabiner.
4. Repeat on every bight.
5. Now, instead of threading the rope multiple times through each bight (as described above), to reinforce the stretcher sides, just clip the rope into each carabiner as you thread your

Fig. 9-4. Completed climbing rope stretcher. The rope has been threaded through each bight and wrapped around itself at the stretcher's head and foot.

way around the stretcher multiple times.

6. Again, at the stretcher's head and foot, wrap the rope around itself to keep the strands together.
7. Repeat the threading process until you have used the entire rope.
8. Tie both sides off using any applicable knot.

This method does, of course, have a few drawbacks: it is gear intensive and therefore heavier. But if you have the people power and resources, it is definitely worth considering.

Sleds

You are in luck if you are traveling with a sled: you already have an improvised litter at your disposal. Although most sleds (whether specifically for mountaineering purposes or a kid's sled) are not the entire body length of a supine adult, they are still effective.

Insulate your patient as best you can, situate her on the sled, and if necessary (depending on the severity of the injuries), secure her onto the sled. You do not want your patient to fall off of the sled while you are transporting her; at the same time, should you lose control you do not want her to get stuck on the sled either.

EVACUATING SOMEONE DOWN A SNOW SLOPE

If you are descending with an improvised litter down snowy terrain, it is extremely important to insulate your patient as best you can. Lying inactive on the snow is a recipe for a quick case of hypothermia.

Place as much insulation as possible under and around the patient.

With enough people power, you can ideally have one to two people controlling the litter from above and another person controlling the litter from below. Regardless of how many rescuers are involved, in sloping terrain the priority lies in controlling the litter from above.

HELICOPTERS AND AIRPLANES

It may be that signaling an aircraft (either from the ground or via a radio, satellite, or cell phone) is your best bet for help or that whoever you contact will in turn summon an aircraft. Presented below are some thoughts on effective signaling and useful aircraft etiquette, which will help the pilot get the job done.

Bringing a helicopter or airplane onto the scene is not a decision to be taken lightly. Flying in a mountain environment can be dangerous for pilots and passengers alike, not to mention the large amount of resources used in conducting this type of rescue.

It is perhaps a misconception, perpetuated by Hollywood stuntmen and -women, that a helicopter can just swoop in and pluck a climber off a wall. Although it is possible, it is a maneuver only made under very specific circumstances and by highly trained teams. The vast majority of aircraft-assisted rescues require the injured party to be brought to the top of the cliff (providing that an adequate landing site exists) or to be on level ground out from the base of the climb.

HELP SIGNAL

Ideally, any signal visible from the air will attract the attention of a pilot flying above: "Help!" in big letters, a flashing signal mirror, a signal fire, and so on. But if you want to play it by the book, thereby avoiding the possibility of misinterpretation, here are a few official signals.

"Help," "SOS," a V (indicates help needed), or an X (indicates medical help needed) can be scratched out in deep troughs in the dirt with sticks and rocks, stamped or dug out in the snow, spelled out with climbing rope, and so on. Colored drink crystals (including hot chocolate), pudding, and gelatin can all be mixed with water and sprinkled over the snow to help define the letters. Remember the difference in scale from the air; a general guideline is that letters be at least 1 foot in width and 8 to 12 feet tall.

You can also lie down on the ground if the suggestions above fail to attract attention. Frantic waving at aircraft sends an unclear message.

OTHER SIGNALING TOOLS

A whistle, signal fire, or mirror can also be used to draw attention to your party.

If using a signal fire, search for a wide-open clearing to build it in. During the day, use a fire's smoke to draw attention to yourself. Carefully adding wet foliage helps produce billowing white smoke, while rubber items (if this is truly an emergency it might be worth parting with that sticky rubber) generate thick black smoke. At night, three fires situated in a triangle signify a call for help.

Although shouting is effective for drawing attention to one's self, the human voice eventually tires. A whistle is much more effective not only for longevity, but for the high-pitched tone it produces—audible over a much larger distance than the human voice. Three sharp blasts indicate a need for help.

A mirror (or anything reflective for that matter) can be effective at communicating over long distances. It is not a foolproof tactic by any means—particularly if the weather is cloudy—but is nonetheless worth having in your bag of tricks. Again, hopefully any sharp glint will be enough to attract the attention of someone flying above (or off at a distance), but to help avoid being missed, here is the SOS pattern: three short flashes, three long flashes, three short flashes.

Once a pilot locates you she may signal you back with a rocking left to right motion, which means, "Signal understood. I will comply."

HELPING THOSE WHO WILL HELP YOU

Time is extremely important in mountain rescue; conditions constantly are changing and pilots are often dealing with flying in tight, narrow spaces with not much of a margin for error. As a party anticipating a rescue, there are several ways in which you can help your pilot prior to her landing:

- If applicable have all medical notes about your patient organized and ready to be handed off (these are called "SOAP notes" in wilderness medicine speak).
- Have a small, lightweight travel bag ready for whoever is being evacuated

containing a warm layer, a small quantity of food and water, and any medications. The pilot may be limited on the amount of weight she can fly out; it is preferable to be organized and prepared with less rather than more.

■ Keep ice axes, ski poles, and other sharp objects separate from your patient's small travel bag. Often pilots will want to stow these separately. If you have extra material available, wrap all sharp points of these objects and secure them with tape. Balled-up socks stuffed onto the points work well.

The bottom line is to follow your pilot (or rescuer's) instructions as best you can. That will be the biggest help overall.

SITE PREPARATION

Find a clear landing site as flat as possible (for a helicopter the landing zone can't have more than a 10 percent grade).

Areas must be clear of wires. Often these are not visible from the air.

Ideally the site will allow the aircraft to drop slightly downward on its take-off (this is more relevant to airplanes than helicopters). This translates into a runway or landing pad that slopes slightly downhill.

For a helicopter, create at least a 100-foot-diameter landing pad.

For an airplane, the runway will depend on the plane's size. In Alaska, most bush planes need a 1000-foot by 50-foot landing strip. (If you are on the snow this means packing out a runway either with snowshoes, skis, or walking up and down ad nauseam. It is a tedious task but it could mean the differ-

ence between being rescued or not).

If you are creating a landing strip on a relatively unfamiliar glacier, take the time to probe for crevasses.

If being rescued on snow, firmly plant large objects (the brighter the color, the better) in the snow along the runway's right side (looking downglacier). Sticks or wands are not large enough; do not use metal objects. Light changes rapidly on snowy surfaces and any sort of additional depth of field you can provide your pilot in flat light can be of great help to her. It can also be helpful to the pilot to hang some sort of wind-direction indicators (any lightweight material tied up off the ground to a ski, stick, small tree, or pole; make sure it is securely tied).

LANDING AND TAKE-OFF

If you have ground-to-air connection with your pilot, provide her with your best estimates on the following details:

■ Air temperature
■ Wind speed and direction
■ Any obstacles in the landing zone
■ Snow conditions if applicable
■ Angle of the landing zone
■ Type of terrain in the landing zone

As the aircraft approaches (and then takes off), make sure that all loose items are secured. Be aware that even small debris kicked up by the aircraft as it lands can be a hazard to uncovered eyes and faces. Also, any sort of long poles (e.g., wands sticking out of your pack, probes, a radio antenna) can be ripped out of your hands by a helicopter's wind.

RESCUE INSURANCE

Rescue insurance is something definitely worth considering; your wallet will thank you. According to Denali National Park, a short evacuation in a helicopter can cost upward of several thousand dollars, not to mention the additional cost of rescue workers. For example, helping an injured climber with a knee tweaked just above the 17,000-foot camp on Denali ended up costing the park $21,750; ground base rescue crews were deployed from the 14,000-foot camp and the patient was then evacuated by helicopter to base camp. Coinciding bad weather compounded the costs. These figures do not even reflect costs to the military for use of their specialized high-altitude helicopters. The American Alpine Club offers climber's insurance with additional high altitude coverage as part of their yearly membership (see *www.americanalpineclub.org*).

The powerful downwash created by a helicopter's rotors in landing and taking off can create a severe drop in temperature, a scenario that has resulted in episodes of frostbite in cold conditions. Dress appropriately if you are in such conditions.

If the helicopter is raising or lowering anything by a line, allow the line to touch down to the ground before you touch it; otherwise you may get shocked with static electricity.

If your pilot is making a night landing, do not shine lights directly at the aircraft.

A few important signals to keep in mind as the aircraft approaches:

- Holding your arms straight out horizontally and flapping them up over your head several times signals "Do not land" to the aircraft (not, "Hey, here we are! We need help!").
- Standing with your back into the wind and arms pointing straight into the landing site signals "Backs are to the wind, land where we are pointing."

Some other things to keep in mind:

Once the helicopter or airplane lands, do not approach until instructed to do so by the pilot. Imagine a clock drawn around the radius of the helicopter or airplane with twelve o'clock at the nose and six o'clock at the tail. It is proper etiquette to approach from between ten and twelve o'clock. The helicopter's back rotor is almost invisible once it is in motion; therefore, it is good practice to not approach helicopters from the back.

If the aircraft lands on a slope, approach and exit from the downhill side.

If you are not needed at the aircraft, stay at least 100 feet away.

Again, time can be of the essence for pilots. Do your best to be as efficient as possible so the pilot can be quickly on her way. There is more than one story out there of Alaska bush pilots sneaking in a glacier landing during a short weather window only to be stuck out on the glacier for the night (or more!) due to quickly changing conditions.

Appendix A: Accident Statistics

Reviewing trends that have either directly caused or contributed to climbing accidents is a valuable learning tool for increasing risk-management and decision-making skills. These figures are courtesy of the 2005 edition of the American Alpine Club's *Accidents in North American Mountaineering*, edited by Jed Williamson.

	1951-03 USA	1959-03 CANADA	2004 USA	2004 CANADA
Terrain				
Rock	4141	503	96	18
Snow	2289	341	46	5
Ice	231	146	18	12
River	14	3	0	0
Unknown	22	9	0	0
Ascent or Descent				
Ascent	2735	555	118	23
Descent	2152	352	40	10
Unknown	247	10	1	2
Other [N.B.]	6	0	1	0
Immediate Cause				
Fall or slip on rock	2887	273	71	10
Slip on snow or ice	915	198	35	7
Falling rock, ice, or object	585	131	16	4
Exceeding abilities	500	29	25	1
Illness [1]	357	25	5	1
Stranded	310	49	13	3
Avalanche	276	120	2	5
Exposure	257	13	7	0
Rappel Failure/Error[2]	252	44	11	1
Loss of control/glissade	185	16	7	0

	1951-03 USA	1959-03 CANADA	2004 USA	2004 CANADA
Immediate Cause (continued)				
Nut/chock pulled out	183	8	8	1
Failure to follow route	164	29	7	0
Fall into crevasse/moat	152	48	1	2
Piton/ice screw pulled out	87	12	7	0
Faulty use of crampons	87	5	5	0
Lightning	45	7	1	0
Skiing[3]	50	10	1	1
Ascending too fast	61	0	3	0
Equipment failure	13	3	1	0
Other [4]	358	34	27	1
Unknown	60	9	1	0
Contributory Causes				
Climbing unroped	960	161	19	2
Exceeding abilities	877	199	4	1
Placed no/inadequate protection	646	94	27	12
Inadequate equipment/clothing	630	68	21	0
Weather	442	63	10	1
Climbing alone	370	67	13	2
No hard hat	304	28	12	1
Nut/chock pulled out	196	31	0	1
Inadequate belay	181	27	9	1
Darkness	134	20	2	0
Poor position	151	20	6	0
Party separated	110	10	3	2
Piton/ice screw pulled out	86	13	0	0
Failure to test holds	89	28	4	3
Exposure	57	13	0	0
Failed to follow directions	71	11	0	0
Illness[1]	39	9	0	0
Equipment failure	11	7	0	0
Other[4]	251	99	5	1
Age of Individuals				
Under 15	123	12	2	0
15-20	1226	202	9	1
21-25	1304	246	33	5
26-30	1208	205	27	3

	1951-03	1959-03	2004	2004
	USA	CANADA	USA	CANADA
Age of Individuals (continued)				
31-35	1011	110	18	2
36-50	1090	136	58	5
Over 50	191	27	15	2
Unknown	1900	504	33	13
Experience Level				
None/Little	1676	294	48	5
Moderate (1 to 3 years)	1494	354	50	0
Experienced	1718	427	79	6
Unknown	1915	511	43	24
Month of Year				
January	202	23	7	2
February	196	51	2	4
March	279	66	13	2
April	381	33	8	5
May	847	55	18	2
June	979	65	30	4
July	1061	244	24	6
August	987	177	15	4
September	1136	70	11	4
October	415	38	20	0
November	175	14	5	2
December	86	24	7	0
Unkknown	17	1	0	0
Type of Injury/Illness (Data since 1984)				
Fracture	1049	206	67	10
Laceration	622	71	35	0
Abrasion	299	75	10	1
Bruise	406	77	27	4
Sprain/strain	281	29	24	2
Concussion	201	28	13	0
Hypothermia	144	15	3	1
Frostbite	112	9	4	0
Dislocation	99	15	10	1
Puncture	42	13	1	0
Acute Mountain Sickness	39	0	1	0
HAPE	65	0	0	0
HACE	23	0	0	0
Other[5]	274	43	20	4
None	184	182	23	6

N.B. Some accidents happen when climbers are at the top or bottom of a route, not climbing. They may be setting up a belay or rappel or are just not anchored when they fall. (This category was created in 2001. We still have "Unknown" because of solo climbers.)

[1] These illnesses/injuries, which led directly or indirectly to the accident, included: AMS, deep vein thrombosis, tooth problems, HAPE, frostbite, and an acute abdomen.

[2] These include no back-up knot—so rappelled off end of ropes, inadequate anchors, rope too short, improper use of descending device, inattention by belayer when lowering.

[3] This category was set up originally for ski mountaineering. Backcountry touring or snowshoeing incidents—even if one gets avalanched—are not in the data.

[4] These include: hand or foothold broke off (10); frostbite (3); unable to self-arrest (7); rope ascender came off; failure to disclose medical condition to guides (2); dislocated shoulder while mantling; rope jammed in crack; carrying ice ax upside down; bee attack; simul-climbing—so too much slack in rope; ice pillar broke off; threw whole rope down—so came undone when weighted; late starts resulting in benighting (2); failure to follow instincts; wet rock (3); leader unable to communicate with belayer (2).

[5] These included: dehydration and exhaustion (5), DVT, rope burns on hands; kidney failure; collapsed lunch; pneumo/hemothorax; heat exhaustion; multiple bee stings; internal injuries; acute abdomen (unknown problem); tooth problems; lightning burns.

Editor's Note: Under the category "other," many of the particular items will have been recorded under a general category. For example, the climber who dislodges a rock that falls on another climber would be coded as Falling Rock/Object, or the climber who has a hand hold come loose and falls would also be coded as Fall On Rock.

A climber disappeared on Mt. Sir Sanford, but no details are known as to whether it was on ascent or descent or what the cause may have been so it is reported as "unknown."

Appendix B: Gear Specifications

Climbing equipment is designed to be both lightweight and strong. However, these goals are often in opposition, so the end result is equipment made strong enough for standard climbing applications, and as light as possible while still allowing for a decent margin of safety. This fact becomes increasingly important when we move out of "normal" recreational use and into the more complex systems and forces seen in rescue situations. To account for this, many SAR teams use heavy-duty gear: steel carabiners and super-fat webbing straps, specialty pulleys and thicker diameter ropes. Carrying gear of this magnitude when recreational climbing is unrealistic, so realize that when you are faced with a more complex rescue an awareness of your gear's strength ratings will help you make educated decisions and construct systems appropriate to the situation.

The manufacturers' specifications that accompany climbing gear often seem confusing and can be difficult to interpret on their own. Check out the rated strength of a climbing rope, webbing, and carabiners—the common links in our systems—then note the strength on a single wired nut, and add a few knots in all the webbing and rope associated with a normal system. It is quickly clear that equipment strength is important, especially considering the forces that can be generated in a rescue.

It is worth noting that there are no North American gear strength standards. Therefore, in the US you could theoretically start making carabiners in your garage and sell them at your local shop. In Europe minimum gear standards do exist: CE standards. A product must meet these CE specifications in order to be sold legally in Europe. Most major climbing gear manufacturers, North American included, make gear that meets CE standards. However, manufacturers may choose not to pursue a CE certification; CE certification involves time and money that many smaller companies can't afford. In fact, most companies perform tests above and beyond that which would be required of them by CE. Beware though: some manufacturer's gear still does not meet the CE requirements. The UIAA also certifies gear to their own standards, though its seal of approval is not mandatory for sale into Europe. Often UIAA tests are more stringent than CE tests.

In this appendix we have compiled minimum CE strength requirements for commonly used climbing gear as well as some basic information to help interpret the terms. To see how strong your gear is check the manufacturer specifications. Often the kN strength rating is stamped or printed on the piece.

DEFINITIONS

KILONEWTON (kN):

- A newton is the amount of force required to accelerate a mass of one kilogram at a rate of one meter per second squared (1 N = 1 kg x 1 m/s2). Force = mass x acceleration. A kilonewton is 1000 newtons
- A kN is an accurate indication of tested strength because it factors in force due to gravity.
- To obtain a more familiar, if not completely accurate, measurement you can use these formulas to convert the metric system to the English system:
  1 kN = 100 kg = 224.8 lb
  X kN x 100 kg = X kg
  X kN x 224.8 lb = X lbf

POUND FORCE (LBF):

- English system equivalent of the kN. Basically pounds, but also indicates force due to gravity.

IMPACT FORCE:

- Amount of stress put on an object as a result of a fall. For a rope or helmet, low impact force is desirable. It indicates that the rope or helmet absorbs some of the stress so the other objects involved—like the climber, protection, or the sharp edge—do not receive the full potential force.

BASIC CONVERSIONS

These numbers are listed in case you want to break out the calculator and start figuring out forces, loads, and so on.

lb		oz		g		kg
2.2	=	35.3	=	1000	=	1 kg
.00022	=	.035	=	1 g	=	.001
.063	=	1 oz	=	28.35	=	.02835
1 lb	=	16	=	453.6	=	.454

in		yd		m		mm
.039	=	.000108	=	.001	=	1 mm
1 in	=	.028	=	.0254	=	25.4
36	=	1 yd	=	.9144	=	914.4
39.37	=	1.093	=	1 m	=	1000

ROCK PROTECTION

Note that the numbers given are from laboratory test conditions. It doesn't matter how strong the piece is if the rock is poor quality. The wire on protection pieces is often the weakest link so, generally, the bigger the wire, the stronger the piece. This includes camming devices.

Wired/slung Nuts and Chocks
CE standard: 2kN (449.6 lbf)

Spring Loaded Camming Device (SCLD)
CE standard: 5kN (1124lbf)

Note: SLCDs vary widely in strength ratings. Some of the very small ones (usually marketed as aid pieces only) do not meet the CE minimum and therefore are not certified. Conversely, many of the larger cams are much stronger than the CE minimum.

BOLTS

Solid Head Sleeve Bolt	Strength/ Medium Rock (lb)*	Strength/Hard Rock (lb)
3/8 in by 3 in	23/32 kN (5200/7200)	25/36 kN (5600/8100)
1/2 in by 33/4 in	33/45 kN (7300/10,000)	44/48 kN (9800/10,700)

* First number is tensile strength and the second is shear strength. Tensile strength is how strong the metal is when a load pulls directly out on it (similar to the slow pull testing used for ropes, cord, and webbing). Shear strength is how strong the shaft of the bolt is when weighted parallel with the rock surface. This test is more relevant as it reflects normal use for bolt anchors and sport climbing bolts.

BOLT HANGERS

UIAA standard: 25 kN

CARABINERS

CE standards	Gate closed (Major Axis)	Gate open	Gate side (Minor Axis)
Oval	18kN	5kN	7kN
D-shaped	20kN	7kN	7kN
HMS (for belaying)	20kN	6kN	7kN

Note: Locking carabiners need to pass the same strength test numbers.

OTHER GEAR

ASCENDERS

CE standards require statically weighting an ascender on a rope to 4 kN five times. The ascenders should not deform or sustain damage and the rope should not sustain damage. Note that all ascender tests are static. Ascenders are not meant to hold dynamic falls.

Synthetic ropes generally fail at less than one-third the rope's strength when force is applied through an ascender. Do not rely on an ascender to hold a dynamic fall. It is not likely that the ascender will break but the rope almost definitely will fail.

HELMETS

To be CE-approved, helmets must pass the following tests:

- a rounded 5 kg weight dropped from 2 m - the measured impact force must be under 10 kN;
- a flat 5 kg weight dropped onto the front of the tilted helmet – the measured impact force must be under 10 kN

- a flat 5 kg weight dropped onto the back of the tilted helmet – the measured impact force must be under 10 kN
- a flat 5 kg weight dropped onto the side of the tilted helmet – the measured impact force must be under 10 kN
- a sharp 3 kg weight dropped from one meter – the result should be less than full penetration
- the chin strap loaded with 500 N - must result in less than 25 millimeter stretch
- a roll-off test that is difficult to explain

Climbing helmets are certified when they protect against objects hitting your head. They are not approved to protect your head when it hits something else. So wearing a CE-approved helmet is no assurance (for your head) against a long pendulum fall into a corner or a 20-foot ground fall. Bike helmets on the other hand are "approved" when they protect your head when it hits

something but not from things hitting your head. Some climbing helmets do have good protection in both areas, though the CE label does not recognize this. No bike, ski, or kayak helmet is CE approved for climbing.

ICE SCREWS

CE approval strength: 10 kN (2248lbf)

An ice screw is only as good as the ice it is placed in.

ICE AXES

Ice axes can have one of two CE strength ratings.

B-rated (Basic) axes have shafts strong enough for general use.

T-rated (Technical) axes are 30 to 40 percent stronger and are designed for heavy abuse, like torquing of the shaft while climbing mixed routes.

Ice axes with interchangeable picks could have a B shaft with a T pick or vice versa.

ROPES & WEBBING:

ROPES AND CORD

In order to be CE certified, rope and cords must pass the following tests described below. (UIAA standards are typically very similar.) All tests are conducted on brand new sections of rope and cord. It's important to recognize that results would differ greatly with used materials. Materials are tested without knots, sharp edges, or other common occurrences that also decrease overall strength.

SINGLE DYNAMIC CLIMBING ROPES

Note: Rope standards do not differ based on a rope's diameter; rather, all single dynamic climbing ropes must pass these minimums in order to receive CE certification.

A sample of rope is placed in the test rig by means of a figure eight knot attached to an 80kg mass on one end and firmly clamped to a fixed anchor on the other. A factor 1.77 drop is then performed every five minutes until the rope fails. A detailed drawing of of the test configuration can be found at *http://www.uiaa.ch /web.test/visual/Safety/SafComPictorials /PictUIAA101-EN892DynamicRopes.pdf*

- Static elongation must be less than 10%.
- Impact force can be no greater than 12 kN (Note this is tested on one initial drop.)
- No fewer than 5 falls held.
- Dynamic elongation cannot exceed 40% on first drop.
- Sheath slippage (either positive or negative) can be no greater than 20mm. The rope is run multiple times through a device that pulls down on the rope's sheath like a circular squeegee.

There is no tensile strength requirement for single dynamic climbing ropes.

ACCESSORY CORD (NYLON)

Multiple tests are run to ensure accurate measurement of a cord's diameter and weight but tensile strength tests are the only type of tests required to measure how cord will perform under load. Cords between 4 and 8 millimeters are tested.

Cord is pulled on a double drum machine that slowly draws the material out in either direction. The breaking point determines the strength rating. 7mm cord must have a strength rating of 9.8 kN and 8 mm cord a rating of 12.8 kN.

WEBBING AND CORD MATERIALS
NYLON WEBBING

One-inch tubular nylon webbing, first put into use during World War II, is cheap, strong, and abrasion-resistant, but is heavier than many of the other material currently on the market (such as Super Tape and HMPE materials, i.e., Dyneema and Spectra). Most climbers reserve nylon webbing for setting up top-rope anchors and they carry short sections of it on multipitch climbs to leave on rappel anchors. Although nylon webbing does not stretch the way a high-stretch (aka dynamic) rope does, it certainly stretches to some degree. It is a common misconception that webbing has no give at all. When weight is applied the webbing (and any type of material used as a runner) elongates, thereby reducing the amount of force the anchor receives.

11/16-INCH WEBBING

Super Tape (one manufacturer's brand name) is a slimmed-down version of 1-inch tubular nylon webbing. It is not as strong as 1-inch tubular, but is lighter and it has a narrower profile and is therefore favored by many climbers. It is resilient and durable, and it also has good friction holding power on a rope for tying friction hitches.

HMPE (DYNEEMA/SPECTRA)

Plastic grocery bags, six-pack carriers, and milk jugs are the not-so-distant cousins of HMPE products like Spectra and Dyneema—exceptionally strong, lightweight, and fairly water-resistant materials popular in the construction of sewn runners. Although remarkably strong, HMPE products do not absorb energy as well as nylon, due to lower elongation (they are not as stretchy). Another downfall is that its slippery nature makes it difficult for it to hold a knot, and knots significantly reduce a HMPE runner's strength, some sources say up to 50 percent. (This is one reason why the runners are sewn. They can indeed be tied; a triple fisherman's knot is recommended to account for the material's slippery properties but is still not ideal.) HMPE also has a very low melting point. The material begins to yield (i.e., deform) at just 67°C. It is therefore not recommended for friction hitches.

ARAMID (KEVLAR/GEMINI CORD)

Many aramid materials, like Gemini cord, contain Kevlar, which make them incredibly strong. At the same time this can be a disadvantage because the cord is not very flexible and is difficult to tie knots in. This type of material is typically reserved for creating

(Continued on next page)

(Continued)

slings for climbing protection (like those used with Hexcentrics). While it can withstand extremely high temperatures (decomposition begins at 500°C). it is neither very abrasion resistant nor does it absorb forces all that well. Its fibers are also more brittle and degrade with flexing and knots.

NYLON CORD

Many climbers carry a 15- to 20-foot piece of small-diameter nylon cord (also called Perlon) or cordelette on their harnesses for rigging multidirectional anchors. It can also double as a useful rescue tool. Although nylon cord is not as strong as some of the other cord or webbing products on the market, it is easy to tie knots in, is light, and is fairly abrasion resistant. Cord smaller than 7 millimeters will certainly hold your weight, though it is not advised for improvisational rescue purposes. Be aware that cord between 4 and 8 millimeters may be UIAA certified (EN 564), but it is not tested for shock absorption or elasticity. Only mass and tensile strength are tested. Many climbing institutions require cordelettes to be at least 7–millimeters thick.

Be wary of the latest and greatest products on the market. Tried and true products work very well; often, newer products will make improvements in one area but may be lacking in another.

Appendix C: Knot Efficiencies

The following information on knot efficiencies and strength-loss percentages is provided for those of you who fancy yourself "tech geeks": people who enjoy getting into the minutia and science of systems. It is by no means necessary to memorize the breaking strength of every single knot known to climbers, but it can be interesting to note comparative strengths. Just understanding the basic concept behind a knot's breaking strength is enough to help you make educated decisions and think critically about the knots you are choosing to tie and why.

A rope's (webbing's or piece of cord's) tensile strength is measured by the rope being pulled in a straight line. This is the scenario in which a rope is the strongest; the fibers inside the rope are all being pulled in a straight line. The minute any change of direction is introduced, the fibers become less efficient; in other words, strength is lost. As the rope curves, the fibers on the outside of the rope elongate while the fibers on the inside of the curve are compressed. When weighted, the elongated fibers hold a greater percentage of the load than the compressed fibers. The tighter this curve, the more unequal the weight distribution

is between the elongated side and the compressed side and the less efficient the rope becomes. That is why typically rope, cord or webbing break on the outside of a knot's radius instead of within it.

For example, tie an overhand on a bight in a dynamic climbing rope and the rope's strength decreases by 32 to 42 percent. Tie a figure eight on a bight instead and the rope's efficiency decreases 23 to 34 percent. The reason for this difference is that the radiuses of an overhand on a bight's curves are tighter than those of a figure eight on a bight. However, as explained in chapter 2, Rescue Knots, there are multiple factors to consider when choosing a knot. Strength is merely a part of the puzzle worth understanding.

When tying a hitch it is worth understanding that the resulting curve will depend on not only the type of hitch but also on the ratio between the diameter of the material being tied and what it is being tied around. A piece of webbing girth-hitched to a piece of cord will have much sharper curves and bunching in it (and thereby a greater loss in strength) compared to a piece of webbing girth-hitched around a large tree. The greater the ratio, the less strength lost; the smaller the ratio, the more strength lost.

Test results vary considerably, perhaps because there are simply *so* many variables. This explains why the figures presented below are ranges instead of exact percentages. A good rule of thumb is that any combination of standard climbing knots will reduce a material's strength by a minimum of about 30 percent.

This information was compiled from the following sources: Geoffrey Budworth's *Illustrated Encyclopedia of Knots*, Craig Luebben's *Knots for Climbers*, Clyde Soles's *Outdoor Knots Book*, and WSCMRT Training's "Basic Ropes and Knots."

TYPE OF TIE	PERCENTAGE OF STRENGTH LOST
No knot (tensile strength of webbing cord, rope)	0 %
LOOPS	
Figure eight on a bight	20–30 %
Figure eight follow-through	19–34 %
In-line figure eight	25%
Butterfly	28–39%
Bowline	26–45%
Double bowline	25–30%
Overhand on a bight	32–42%
Overhand on a bight (tied in webbing)	32–42%
Figure eight on a bight (tied in webbing)	30%
HITCHES	
Clove hitch	35–45%
Girth hitch	30-60%
Two half hitches	35–40%
BENDS	
Water knot (tied in webbing)	30–40%
Double fisherman's	20–35%
Flemish bend	19–30%

Appendix D: Continuing Education

These organizations provide training and valuable publications should you want to continue learning skills pertinent to the field of rescue (like first-aid training), find groups with which to practice your techniques, or take your skills to the next level.

The American Alpine Club
710 10th Street, Suite 100
Golden, CO 80401
(303) 384-0110
www.americanalpineclub.org
The American Alpine Club (AAC), in operation since 1902, is the United States' national mountaineering and climbing organization. Each year the AAC publishes *Accidents in North American Mountaineering*, the *American Alpine Journal*, and the quarterly *American Alpine News*.

The Alpine Club of Canada
PO Box 8040, Indian Flats Road
Canmore, AB
Canada T1W 2T8
(403) 678-3200
www.alpineclubofcanada.ca
The Alpine Club of Canada (ACC) is Canada's national mountaineering organization and has been a focal point for Canadian mountaineering since 1906. The ACC's website contains a variety of interesting and informative technical articles.

American Mountain Guides Association
Physical address:
1209 Pearl Street, Suites 12 and 14
Boulder, CO 80302

Mailing address:
PO Box 1739
Boulder, CO 80306
(303) 271-0984
www.amga.com
The American Mountain Guides Association (AMGA), founded in 1979, provides support and education to American mountain guides and establishes standards for guiding. The AMGA maintains a database of AMGA-certified guides around the country and affiliated guiding companies.

Association of Canadian Mountain Guides
Box 8341
Canmore, AB
Canada T1W 2V1
(403) 678-2885
www.acmg.ca

Training and Certification Programs
University College of the Caribou
Box 3010
Kamloops, BC
Canada V2C 5N3
(250) 372-0118
Like the AMGA, the Association of Canadian Mountain Guides is a trade and education association for professional mountain guides.

Cordage Institute
994 Old Eagle School Road, Suite 1019
Wayne, PA 19087
(610) 971-4854
www.ropecord.com
The Cordage Institute is an international association of manufacturers, producers, and resellers of cordage, rope, and twine. The institute is involved in the development of standards and guidelines and also publishes a technical manual, *The Ropecord News*, and documents about the safe use of cordage and rope.

International Critical Incident Stress Foundation Inc.
www.icisf.org
This website provides links, articles, and even a hotline number for people struggling with the aftermath of a traumatic event.

International Technical Rescue Symposium
C/O National Association for Search and Rescue
PO Box 232020
Centreville, VA 20120
877-893-0702
www.nasar.org/nasar/conferences
.php?id=146

The International Technical Rescue Symposium (ITRS) is an annual gathering of people involved in all disciplines of rescue, including mountain rescue.

Mountain Rescue Association
PO Box 880868
San Diego, CA 92168
www.mra.org
The Mountain Rescue Association (MRA), formed in 1958, shares information to improve patient care in the mountains and to improve SAR techniques. It is an excellent resource and informational tool for those interested in learning more about organized rescue.

National Association for Search and Rescue
PO Box 232020
Centreville, VA 20120
877-893-0702
www.nasar.org
The National Association for Search and Rescue (NASAR) is dedicated to advancing professional, literary, and scientific knowledge in fields related to search and rescue.

Petzl America
PO Box 160447
Clearfield, UT 84016
(801) 926-1500
en.petzl.com/petzl/Accueil
Petzl, a climbing, caving, canyoneering, and technical-rescue gear manufacturer, provides valuable information on their website and in catalogs about roped climbing and rescue. Their website also includes a "fall factor simulator."

Rigging for Rescue
PO Box 745324
5th Street
Ouray, CO 81427
(970) 325-4474
www.riggingforrescue.com
Rigging for Rescue provides technical rescue workshops emphasizing critical thinking about the statistics and dynamics of rigging, all backed by physics and testing.

Sterling Rope Company
31 Washington Avenue
Scarborough, ME 04074
(207) 885-0330
www.sterlingrope.com
Sterling Rope Company's website offers useful information on rope care, strength, and safe application.

Wilderness Medical Associates
189 Dudley Road
Bryant Pond, ME 04219
888-WILDMED
www.wildmed.com
Wilderness Medical Associates has been teaching courses since 1978 in wilderness emergency situations, rescue, SAR, disaster, and mass casualty, all focused on providing care in a wilderness context.

Wilderness Medical Society
5390 N Academy Boulevard, Suite 310
Colorado Springs, CO 80918
(719) 572-9255
www.wms.org
The Wilderness Medical Society (WMS) is a trade organization for physicians and health professionals. The society publishes a peer-reviewed medical journal, a quarterly newsletter, and an educational presentation series on wilderness medicine topics.

Wilderness Medicine Institute
C/O National Outdoor Leadership School
284 Lincoln Street
Lander, WY 82520
(866) 831-9001
www.nols.edu
The Wilderness Medicine Institute (WMI) offers classes focusing on elements of first aid and emergency medicine unique to wilderness travelers.

Wilderness Risk Managers Conference
NOLS Professional Training
284 Lincoln Street
Lander, WY 82520
(307) 332-8100
www.nols.edu/wrmc/
The Wilderness Risk Managers Conference is held every fall with the goal of helping wilderness enthusiasts and professionals share information on important developments in the field of risk management and wilderness adventure.

Appendix E: Recommended Reading

The following books and magazines can help you further your technical-rescue knowledge as well as develop climbing, critical-thinking, and wilderness medicine skills. Having these skills is an important component in lessening the chance of needing a rescue in the first place. Many of these books were also used as references in writing this book.

ACCIDENTS

American Alpine Club. *Accidents in North American Mountaineering*. Golden, CO: American Alpine Club Press. Published annually.

CLIMBING AND MOUNTAINEERING TECHNIQUES

Chouinard, Yvon. *Climbing Ice*. San Francisco: Sierra Club Books, 1978.

Cox, Steven M., and Kris Fulsaas, eds. *Mountaineering: The Freedom of the Hills*. 7th ed. Seattle: The Mountaineers Books, 2003.

Gadd, Will. *Ice and Mixed Climbing: Modern Technique*. Seattle: The Mountaineers Books, 2003.

Houston, Charles. *Going Higher*. 5th ed. Seattle: The Mountaineers Books, 2005.

Houston, Mark, and Kathy Cosley. *Alpine Climbing: Techniques to Take You Higher*. Seattle: The Mountaineers Books, 2004.

Long, John. *How to Rock Climb: More Climbing Anchors*. Evergreen, CO: Chockstone Press, 1996.

Long, John, and Craig Luebben. *How to Rock Climb: Advanced Rock Climbing*. Helena, MT: Falcon, 1997.

Long, John, and John Middendorf. *How to Rock Climb: Climbing Big Walls*. Evergreen, CO: Chockstone Press, 1994.

Lowe, Jeff. *Ice World: Techniques and Experiences of Modern Ice Climbing*. Seattle: The Mountaineers Books, 1996.

Luebben, Craig. *How to Rappel*. Guilford, CT: Globe Pequot/Falcon, 2000.

——. *Rock Climbing: Mastering Basic Skills*. Seattle: The Mountaineers Books, 2004.

March, Bill. *Modern Rope Techniques in Mountaineering*. Cumbria, England: Cicerone Press, 1990.

Pesterfield, Heidi. *Traditional Lead Climbing: Surviving the Learning Years*. Berkeley: Wilderness Press, 2002.

Powers, Phil. *NOLS Wilderness Mountaineering*. Mechanicsburg, PA: Stackpole Books, 1993.

Twight, Mark, and James Martin. *Extreme Alpinism, Climbing Light, High, and Fast.* Seattle: The Mountaineers Books, 1999.

EQUIPMENT AND KNOTS

Ashley, Clifford. *The Ashley Book of Knots.* New York: Doubleday, 1944.

Budworth, Geoffrey. *The Illustrated Encyclopedia of Knots.* New York: The Lyons Press, 2002.

Luebben, Craig. *Knots for Climbers.* 2nd ed. Guilford, CT: Globe Pequot, 2002.

Soles, Clyde. *The Outdoor Knots Book.* Seattle: The Mountaineers Books, 2004.

———. *Rock and Ice Gear: Equipment for the Vertical World.* Seattle: The Mountaineers Books, 2000.

WSCMRT Training. "Basic Ropes and Knots." *www.western.edu/wscmrt/docs/pdf/trng_rope.pdf.*

FIRST AID AND WILDERNESS MEDICINE

Hackett, Peter, MD. *Mountain Sickness, Prevention, Recognition, and Treatment.* Golden, CO: American Alpine Club Press, 1980.

Schimelpfenig, Tod, and Linda Lindsey. *NOLS Wilderness First Aid.* Mechanicsburg, PA: Stackpole Books, 1991.

Tilton, Buck. *Backcountry First Aid and Extended Care.* 4th ed. Guilford, CT: Globe Pequot, 2002.

Wilkerson, James. *Medicine for Mountaineering and Other Wilderness Activities.* 6th ed. Seattle: The Mountaineers Books, 2009.

RESCUE DEBRIEFING AND TRAUMA RESPONSE

Conover, K. C. "Wilderness EMT Curriculum: Stress Management and Critical Incident Stress Debriefing." Syllabus, Appalachian Search and Rescue Conference, Pittsburgh, PA, 1990.

Mitchell, J. "Development and Functions of a Critical Stress Debriefing Team." *Journal of Emergency Medical Services* 12, no. 12 (1988): 42–46.

Rothschild, Babette. *The Body Remembers.* New York: W. W. Norton, 2000.

RESCUE TECHNIQUES

Fasulo, David. *How to Rock Climb: Self-Rescue.* Helena, MT: Falcon, 1997.

Frank, James A., and Jerrold B. Smith. *CMC Rope Rescue Manual.* Santa Barbara, CA: CMC Rescue Inc., 1992.

Lipke, Rick. *Technical Rescue Riggers Guide.* Bellingham, WA: Conterra Inc., 1998.

Smith, Bruce, and Allen Padgett. *On Rope: North American Vertical Rope Techniques.* Rev. ed. Huntsville, AL: National Speleological Society, 1996.

Tyson, Andy. *Glacier Mountaineering: An Illustrated Guide to Glacier Travel and Crevasse Rescue.* 2nd ed. Carbondale, CO: *Climbing Magazine,* 2004.

Vines, Tom, and Steve Hudson. *High Angle Rescue Techniques.* 2nd ed. St. Louis: Mosby, 1999.

Glossary

ascension rig – a combination of cords or mechanical ascenders that allow a climber to move up a rope. Common names include: Prusik rig (generally two cords – one called a waist Prusik and the other called a foot Prusik); ascender rig uses mechanical ascenders instead of Prusik hitches.

belay escape – a series of steps that allow the belayer to move and tie off the belay to an anchor so that he is free to enact a rescue. The belayed climber's position is maintained on the rope.

belay loop – a sewn loop on most harnesses that is the main connection point between the harness and the leg loops.

bend – a tie that joins the ends of a piece of material together either to form a continuous loop or links two pieces of material together. The tail ends exit the knot in opposite directions.

bight – like a half circle; there is an obvious curve in the rope, but the rope strands do not cross one another.

brake strand – the side of rope breaking a climber's fall–the strand that will be fed through a belay device to lower a climber.

clipping-in short – tying or clipping into the rope at waypoints to reduce the amount of slack in the system; commonly used while ascending a line.

cordelette – a piece of perlon or cord that is generally approximately 7 millimeters in diameter. Its length varies - generally around 10 – 25 feet though it can be shorter.

counterbalance rappelling – using the injured climber's weight on one side of the rope to counterbalance the rescuer's weight for a quick rappel.

cow's tail – a short sling girth hitched to the belay loop; used for attaching to an anchor, setting up a tandem rappel, and rappelling.

cross-loading – loading a carabiner across its short axis: across the gate and spine. This is a much weaker orientation for a carabiner.

crux – the hardest part of a climb; may be only a few moves or it can be longer. A climb is generally rated for the difficulty of its crux.

cyclical loading – the repeated weighting and unweighting of a piece of cordage or webbing.

daisy chain – sewn-webbing leash that a climber uses to attach himself to an anchor or aid pieces. Depending on the style of construction a daisy is generally not made to hold more than body weight.

directional anchor – an anchor that is good for holding a load in one direction.

dressed knot – a tie that does not have any kinks or loose or unnecessarily twisted portions. It has also been "set" or snugged-down with a good tug prior to loading.

dynamic rope – a nylon rope that absorbs force by stretching when loaded.

Dyneema – *See* HMPE.

emergency procedures – organizational framework used to deal with emergency situations.

figure nine – a figure eight on a bight with an additional wrap around the eight's center.

fireman's belay – a back-up belay for rappelling.

fixed-line ascension – climbing a rope that has been anchored at the top and sometimes the bottom. Friction hitches or mechanical ascenders are used to grab the rope and move up or down it.

foot Prusik – a piece of cord that is attached to the rope with a friction hitch. It is long enough to put a foot in and stand up. Used as part of an ascension rig.

foot wraps – wrapping the rope around your foot for friction.

force – the capacity to do work or cause physical change; a vector quantity.

French-freeing – pulling on a piece of climbing gear to help upward progress. Considered poor free climbing style, but useful for quickly getting up challenging sections when time is important.

friction hitches – a type of tie that, when tied around a rope, grabs and holds fast to that specific spot on the line even when weighted.

hands-free – tying off the belay so that the rescuer is able to let go of the belay strand, allowing him to use both hands for another task.

hitch – a tie that has to be tied around something to maintain its form.

HMPE – an exceptionally strong, lightweight and fairly water-resistant material used in making sewn runners. The downsides of HMPE are that its slippery nature makes it a poor choice for knots and it has a very low melting point, so it is generally not recommended friction hitches.

kiloNewton – the amount of force required to accelerate a mass of 1000 kilograms at a rate of one meter per second squared (1 kN = 1000 kg x 1 m/s2).

leap-frog – to use one piece of gear as protection while moving the previous protection piece forward to protect the next move.

kN – *See* kiloNewton.

leg wraps – wrapping the belay strand around the leg to substitute for the break hand. This allows the climber to be hands-free.

lfb – *See* pound force.

load strand – whichever strand of rope is actively holding the load (e.g., the climber).

locking-assist belay device – a belay device, such as the Petzl GriGri or Trango Cinch, that automatically locks onto the rope in the event of a fall.

loop – a tie that forms a continuous circle and can be tied anywhere along a rope. A loop can also be created without a knot in which case it is like a bight except that the rope strands do cross and the circle is closed.

master point – the main connection point for attaching anything to an anchor.

mechanical advantage – a system that spreads work out over time and distance to reduce the amount of force necessary to complete a task.

mechanical ascenders – a climbing device that

MMO – abbreviation for Munter-mule-overhand.

MP – abbreviation for Master Point.

multidirectional anchor – an anchor constructed to hold a load in multiple directions. Most often constructed in multipitch climbing in which an anchor must be able to resist a downward pull as well as upward or sideways pulls.

multiplying advantage – stacking mechanical advantage systems; for example a 2:1 acts on a 3:1 thus creating a 6:1.

Munter-mule – two hitches commonly tied together; the Munter is used to belay a line and the mule is used to tie off the Munter.

PMMO – abbreviation for Prusik-Munter-mule-overhand.

PMP – Prusik-minding pulleys.

pound force – the English units equivalent of the kiloNewton.

prusiking – using friction hitches to ascend a rope. Generally the climber uses a waist Prusik and a foot Prusik for his ascension system

pulley point –the moving pulley in a 3:1 system.

pulley system – *See* raising system.

raising system – a mechanical advantage system created to lift an object.

rappel backup – a safety backup to a climber's rappel break hand. If the climber is incapacitated on his rappel or he removes his break hand from the rope for any reason he will stop on the rope rather than sliding to the bottom (or off the ends).

ratchet – a device used to restrict motion in one direction.

redirectional piece – a piece of gear used to redirect the rope.

releasable hitch – a hitch that can be released while under load, generally without causing the system to fail.

rescue loop – a short loop of 7-millimeter cord tied with a Flemish bend or double fisherman's.

rescue pulley – a wheeled pulley used for rescue purposes.

rescue spider – a way to tie a cordelette that allows easy anchor-to-rappel transitions and security for tandem rappelling.

rope solo – a rope system to protect solo climbing.

self-blocking belay device – a belay device that can be set up to block or trap the rope in the event of a fall. The belayer can let go of his brake hand without compromising the belay.

self-tending ratchet – a friction hitch attached to the main hauling line that captures the gain of the raised load.

shear strength – resistance of a material to side force that would cause it to split and slide past itself.

shelf – secondary anchor clip-in point. It is above the master point, but still redundant if constructed properly.

short roping – a guiding technique used to assist a challenged climber through exposed terrain.

simul-climbing – a rope system allowing two or more climbers to climb at the same time, including the leader.

Spectra- *See* HMPE.

static rope – a rope that is constructed to be low-stretch. Generally the rope absorbs less force and therefore transfers more of that force to the anchors or climber.

tandem rappelling – two people attached together and rappelling on the same lines.

tensile strength – the resistance of a material to a force that is pulling or tearing it apart.

tension release hitch – *See* releasable hitch.

tether – a short sling or section of rope used to attach something (for example, a climber) to an anchor.

third hand – a piece of cord that is tied onto the rope with a friction hitch and clipped to the harness, used as a backup to a climber's brake hand on rappel.

triaxial loading – loading a carabiner in three directions. Carabiners are designed to be loaded in two directions along their longest axis; triaxial loading greatly reduces a carabiner's strength.

tubular belay device – a common style of belay device (e.g., ATC, Tuber, Stich-plate, Pyramid, etc.).

waist Prusik – *See* ascension rig.

working end – the side of the rope leading to the anchor, the inactive climber, or simply the end that runs into the rope bag.

Index

Another beautiful day in the mountains!

About the Authors

Molly Loomis and Andy Tyson are international mountain guides. Their work, personal expeditions and travels have led them to crags and ranges around North America, and farther-flung places like Patagonia, Kyrgyzstan, Russia, Nepal, Bhutan, China, South Korea, India, and Antarctica. Together they bring more than twenty-five years of guiding and instructing experience to this book. Both also volunteer on their local search and rescue team. Andy is the author of *Glacier Mountaineering*, published by *Climbing* magazine, while Molly has published articles in publications such as *Rock and Ice, Climbing, Alpinist,* and the *American Alpine Journal*. Upcoming climbing adventures include returning to Antartica and the eastern Himalaya; they also enjoy spending time at their home in the Tetons.

The UIAA encourages the inclusion of information in guidebooks that helps visitors from overseas to understand the most important information about local access, grades and emergency procedures. The UIAA also encourages climbers and mountaineers to share knowledge and views on issues such as safety, ethics, and good practice in mountain sports. The UIAA is not responsible for, and accepts no liability for, the technical content or accuracy of the information in this guidebook. Climbing, hill walking and mountaineering are activities with a danger of personal injury and death. Participants should be aware of, understand and accept these risks and be responsible for their own actions and involvement.

THE MOUNTAINEERS, founded in 1906, is a nonprofit outdoor activity and conservation club, whose mission is "to explore, study, preserve, and enjoy the natural beauty of the outdoors. . . . " Based in Seattle, Washington, the club is now one of the largest such organization in the United States, with seven branches throughout Washington State.

The Mountaineers sponsors both classes and year-round outdoor activities in the Pacific Northwest, which include hiking, mountain climbing, ski-touring, snowshoeing, bicycling, camping, kayaking, nature study, sailing, and adventure travel. The club's conservation division supports environmental causes through educational activities, sponsoring legislation, and presenting informational programs.

All club activities are led by skilled, experienced instructors, who are dedicated to promoting safe and responsible enjoyment and preservation of the outdoors.

If you would like to participate in these organized outdoor activities or the club's programs, consider a membership in The Mountaineers. For information and an application, write or call The Mountaineers, Club Headquarters, 7700 Sand Point Way NE, Seattle, WA 98115; 206-521-6001. You can also visit the club's website at *www.mountaineers.org* or contact The Mountaineers via email at *clubmail@mountaineers.org.*

The Mountaineers Books, an active, nonprofit publishing program of the club, produces guidebooks, instructional texts, historical works, natural history guides, and works on environmental conservation. All books produced by The Mountaineers Books fulfill the club's mission.

Send or call for our catalog of more than 500 outdoor titles:

The Mountaineers Books
1001 SW Klickitat Way, Suite 201
Seattle, WA 98134
800-553-4453
mbooks@mountaineersbooks.org
www.mountaineersbooks.org

 The Mountaineers Books is proud to be a corporate sponsor of The Leave No Trace Center for Outdoor Ethics, whose mission is to promote and inspire responsible outdoor recreation through education, research, and partnerships. The Leave No Trace program is focused specifically on human-powered (nonmotorized) recreation.

Leave No Trace strives to educate visitors about the nature of their recreational impacts, as well as offer techniques to prevent and minimize such impacts. Leave No Trace is best understood as an educational and ethical program, not as a set of rules and regulations.

For more information, visit *www.LNT.org,* or call 800-332-4100.

MORE CLIMBING TITLES FROM THE TOP ATHLETES AND ORGANIZATIONS IN THE SPORT:

Mountaineering: The Freedom of the Hills, 8th Ed.
The Mountaineers
The all-time best selling standard reference for
the sport of climbing.

**Alpine Climbing: Techniques
to Take You Higher**
Kathy Cosley and Mark Houston

**Big Wall Climbing:
Elite Technique**
Jared Ogden
Skills and strategies unique to big walls.

**Ice and Mixed Climbing:
Modern Technique**
Will Gadd
Expand your climbing chops with
instructions from the best.

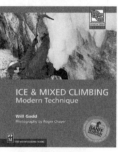

Rock Climbing: Mastering Basic Skills, 2nd Ed.
Topher Donahue and Craig Luebben
For beginner to intermediate climbers.

**Gym Climbing: Maximizing
Your Indoor Experience**
Matt Burbach
Urban climbing for new climbers, climbers
staying in shape and climbers who find all the
challenge they desire indoors.

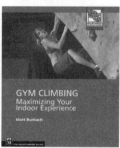

Climbing: Training for Peak Performance, 2nd Ed.
Clyde Soles
Build the muscles you need for this ultimate
of muscle-powered sports.

Climbing: Expedition Planning
Clyde Soles and Phil Powers
How to organize climbing trips
from small to large groups.

THE MOUNTAINEERS BOOKS